# The Ashrafiya Hymn

The Story of the Last Prophet

**Dr. Ashi Ezz**

Copyright © 2024 by Dr. Ashi Ezz

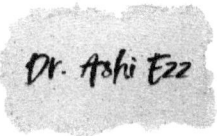

Thank you for purchasing an authorized edition of this book. Copyright fuels creativity, encourages diverse voices, promotes free speech, and contributes to a vibrant culture. By complying with copyright laws and not reproducing, scanning, or distributing any part of this book in any form without permission, you are supporting writers and allowing the continuation of publishing works for every reader.

First edition

Paperback ISBN: 978-1-0670520-1-0

Kindle & EPUB ISBN: 978-1-0670520-0-3

Audio ISBN: 978-1-0670520-2-7

While the author has made every effort to provide accurate Internet addresses at the time of publication, neither the author nor the publisher assumes any responsibility for errors or changes that occur after publication. The author also does not have any control over and does not assume any responsibility for third-party websites or their content.

For inquiries, further information, please contact:

Email: ashiezzpublish@gmail.com

## Contents

Introduction ............................................................. 1

Section 1: The Light of His Biography ....................... 5

Section 2: The Light of His Virtues .......................... 53

Section 3: Glimpse of His Daily life ........................ 79

Section 4: Some of His Miracles ............................. 90

Section 5: The Light of His Being ......................... 106

The Book Cover ..................................................... 122

Acknowledgments ................................................. 123

References ............................................................ 124

# Dedication

In the name of Allah[1] and only for the sake of Him, this book I lay, in honor of His Messenger, the light of our way. Prophet Muhammad[2], peace and blessings be upon him, the finest example humanity has ever known. In the Qur'an[3], a call so clear, to love him more than all we hold dear, to follow his path with unwavering devotion. This work is my humble effort to reflect that love and reveal to the world who he truly is through poetry.

This book is not a source of halal or haram, nor a guide for learning Islamic religious law. Although I have strived to translate the meanings with care, I encourage you to seek refuge in the Quran's light and the authentic Hadith's guiding might. Return to their profound Arabic words, for there lies the ultimate clarity. Let this serve as a humble reflection, always pointing towards the truest direction.

In offering this work, I seek only Allah's pleasure and hope to ignite a deeper connection between you and the man who was truly sent as a mercy for all. If I am correct, it is from Allah, and if I am wrong, it is from myself and Shaytan. Allah and His Messenger are blameless from my errors.

---

[1] Allah: The Arabic word for God, representing the one and only deity in Islam, embodying supreme power, mercy, and unity.
[2] Muhammad: The final prophet in Islam, revered as the messenger of Allah, who brought the Quran and exemplified a life of compassion, justice, and devotion.
[3] Qur'an: The holy book of Islam, believed to be the literal word of Allah as revealed to Prophet Muhammad (PBUH), guiding Muslims in all aspects of life.

# Introduction

In a world yearning for hope, kindness, and guidance, there walked a man whose every step was a blessing. He was Muhammad, peace and blessings be upon him, the best whoever walked the earth, sent as a mercy to all creation. His words were a balm for the weary, his actions a lighthouse for the lost, and his presence a living testament to God's infinite compassion.

He was not just a leader of men, but a heart that beat for humanity. His life, like a brilliant dawn after a long, dark night, illuminated the path of truth, justice, and mercy. Through him, God fulfilled His divine promise:

---

**"And We have not sent you, [O Muhammad], except as a mercy to the worlds."**

(Qur'an 21:107)

---

This collection of poetry is a humble tribute to his life; a life woven with mercy and love to all human being. These verses do not simply recount historical events; they are meant to bring you into the moments when hearts broke at his final farewell, when his hands lifted in prayer for his people, and when his smile melted the hardest of souls.

God describes him:

> *"Indeed, there has come to you a Messenger from among yourselves. Grievous to him is what you suffer; [he is] concerned over you, and to the believers is kind and merciful."*
>
> *(Qur'an 9:128)*

In every verse, you will feel the weight of his care for mankind, the depth of his love for the broken-hearted, and the strength he lent to those in despair. Each poem is a glimpse into the immense legacy he left behind, for he was the embodiment of divine mercy, a beacon of light whose influence ripples through time.

With each page, we invite you to journey closer to his heart, to relive the moments of joy and sorrow, victory and loss, as if you were standing among his companions, listening to his final words. May your heart be moved, your soul awakened, and your love for the Beloved grow deeper with every word.

For truly, he was, and will forever be, the best of creation "Ashraf[4] Al-Khalq", Peace and blessings be

---

[4] Ashraf: is an Arabic name meaning "the most honorable one" and it is one of the names of the Prophet Muhammad (PBUH) and is also used for individuals who are descendants of his bloodline.

upon him, our beloved Muhammad; the mercy to all the worlds.

**Why This Book Was Written**

Having introduced the Seal of Prophets in my book "Muhammad: Lasting Resilience Model", I was advised to offer a glimpse of his life, a portrait of his grace. I thought; what better way to honor such a noble face than through the timeless art of poetic verse; beauty unveiled through beauty's embrace.

Additionally, in recent times, Prophet Muhammad, peace and blessings be upon him, has been the target of criticism from people who don't truly understand him. These attacks often stem from a lack of knowledge, not malice. This book wasn't written as a defense but as an invitation; a humble attempt to give readers a clearer understanding of who he really was.

Just as the sun is essential to the planets and water sustains fish, the Prophet's influence is vital to the hearts and souls of those who know him. Through these poems, I aim to introduce his true nature to a broader audience. His life wasn't just about the past; it carries timeless lessons on leadership, compassion, and resilience that continue to inspire.

By working on something connected to him, we allow his wisdom to shine through and illuminate the darkness of misunderstanding. This book is my small effort to show the world the man who was sent as a mercy to all. Through these verses, my hope is that readers catch a glimpse of his immense impact and begin to see him not as a distant figure, but as a guide whose presence is still deeply relevant today.

Of all the tributes written about him, none has moved me more than a piece by Hassan ibn Thabit, one of the Prophet's closest companions. His words capture the essence of their bond; the deep reverence, the willingness to sacrifice, and the love that transcended all worldly attachments. Here's my translation of his unforgettable lines:

> *"My eyes have never seen a soul so true,*
> *No woman birthed a beauty like you.*
> *In form and grace, you have no flaw,*
> *As if you shaped yourself by your own law."*

This book unfolds in five sections, each a section of light. The first, a glimpse of his life so bright. The second reveals his virtues pure, a mirror of morals that forever endure. The third shares his days, his deeds, his way, with companions close, in work and play. The fourth collects his miracles divine, signs of his truth, a celestial sign. And last, a poem picture; a portrait sublime of him as you see, beyond space and time.

My prayer is that through these words, you will come to love and follow him with the same devotion that his companions did.

# Section 1: The Light of His Biography

## *The Noble Lineage of the Prophet Muhammad Pbuh*

*In Mecca's[5] heart, beneath the desert sky,*
*The Prophet's birth, a tale that will not die.*

*God chose for him the purest family line,*
*A lineage blessed, by purpose made divine.*
*Through Adam's sons, a light began to gleam,*
*Through Abraham[6], fulfilled was God's great scheme.*
*From Ismail's[7] seed, the chosen path was laid,*
*Through Kinanah's[8] tribe, the message was conveyed.*

*From Quraysh[9]'s noble roots, there came to rise*
*The brightest star to grace all earthly skies.*
*Within Bani Hashim's[10] walls, he drew first breath,*
*A soul of mercy, life, and hope in death.*

---

[5] Mecca: A sacred city in Saudi Arabia, the birthplace of Prophet Muhammad (PBUH) and the holiest site in Islam.

[6] Abraham: A revered prophet and patriarch, considered the father of monotheism in Islam, Christianity, and Judaism.

[7] Ismail: The son of Prophet Abraham (PBUH), honored in Islam for his faith and patience, and believed to have helped build the Kaaba in Mecca.

[8] Kinanah: An ancient Arab tribe, known as the ancestors of the Quraysh, the tribe of Prophet Muhammad (PBUH).

[9] Quraysh: The dominant tribe of Mecca during Prophet Muhammad's (PBUH) time, guardians of the Kaaba and his noble lineage.

[10] Bani Hashim: A respected clan of the Quraysh tribe, renowned for its nobility and generosity, and the family of Prophet Muhammad (PBUH).

"The best of best," his truth with humble tone,
No boast he made; God's choosing, his alone.

Through every branch, the finest fruit was grown,
And from this line, a legacy was shown.
A man unmatched, in kindness and in grace,
In every deed, a light for time and space.

God shaped his life with wisdom in each part,
And placed within a strong yet tender heart.
No pride he bore, yet greatness marked his name,
The highest rank, untouched by worldly fame.

In him, the finest traits of humankind,
A leader, guide, with heart and mind aligned.
Through his pure lineage, shining ever bright,
God sent to us the mercy of His light.

## *The Path of His Nobel Name*

*Through ancient paths where lineage shines so bright,*
*A noble line adorned with holy light.*

*Muhammad ibn[11] Abdullah[12], name so clear,*
*Ibn Abdul-Muttalib, held most dear.*
*Ibn Hashim, of noble tribe and fame,*
*Through Abd Manaf, a pure and honored name.*

*A lineage pure, in every branch refined,*
*Each name a jewel, in time's great chain aligned.*

*Ibn Qusayy, the keeper of the door,*
*Ibn Kilab, whose name the Quraysh bore.*
*Ibn Murrah, the link in sacred thread,*
*Ibn Ka'b, whose words of honor spread.*

*Ibn Lu'ayy, through generations wide,*
*Ibn Ghalib, where noble blood resides.*
*Ibn Fihr, the founder of the clan,*
*Ibn Malik, a name revered by man.*

*Through generations guarded, safe, and true,*
*The path prepared for what the world would view.*

---

[11] Ibn: An Arabic term meaning "son of," used in names to indicate lineage or ancestry.
[12] Abdullah, the father of Prophet Muhammad (PBUH), means "Servant of Allah," reflecting devotion and humility. His lineage includes other noble Arabic names up to Ibrahim (Abraham) as mentioned above.

*Ibn al-Nadr, whose grace did never cease,*
*Ibn Kinana, of noble peace.*
*Ibn Khuzaymah, whose heart did shine,*
*Ibn Mudrikah, in lineage divine.*

*Ibn Ilyas, the bridge from age to age,*
*Ibn Mudar, a wisdom to engage.*
*Ibn Nizar, the strength of ancient line,*
*Ibn Ma'ad, with roots both deep and fine.*

*Ibn Adnan, the one whose soul did glow,*
*A prophet's birth from this great line did flow.*
*From Ismail's seed, God's plan was made complete,*
*And Ibrahim, whose legacy we greet.*

*And here we have it, his full name in light:*
*Muhammad ibn Ibrahim, pure and bright.*

*In Muhammad, the chosen and the blessed,*
*The final light, above all time, confessed.*
*No path more noble, no name more true,*
*A destiny profound, in every hue.*

*Let all the earth remember and acclaim,*
*Muhammad's lineage, and his holy name.*
*For through his birth, the world was shown the way,*
*A light eternal, brightening night and day.*

## *Born in the Year of the Elephant*

*The Year of the Elephant[13] marked the day,*
*When armies came, with doom to lay.*
*But God's great power made them fall,*
*Protecting Kaaba[14], standing tall.*

*An orphan born, his father gone,*
*In six short years, his mother drawn.*
*To God, he looked, his only guide,*
*Divine care stayed close by his side.*

*His grandfather's arms held him near,*
*But soon he too would disappear.*
*To Abu Talib's [15]home he went,*
*With love and care, his days were spent.*

*Yet through it all, God's plan was clear,*
*The orphan boy had none to fear.*
*In valleys vast, he was raised,*
*With courage, strength, his spirit blazed.*

---

[13] The Year of the Elephant: The year 570 CE, when an army led by the Abyssinian ruler Abraha attempted to destroy the Kaaba in Mecca, but was miraculously thwarted, marking the birth year of Prophet Muhammad (PBUH).

[14] Kaaba: The sacred cubic structure in Mecca, considered the holiest site in Islam, towards which Muslims direct their prayers. It is believed to have been built by Prophet Abraham (PBUH) and his son Ismail (PBUH).

[15] Abu Talib: The uncle of Prophet Muhammad (PBUH), who protected and supported him during his early years, despite not embracing Islam.

*Halima[16], blessed, took him in,*
*Her heart was moved by fate's soft spin.*
*An orphan child, yet rich in grace,*
*She found in him a light, a place.*

*The winds of Mecca carried far,*
*This child of prophecy, a star.*
*Born in the year of God's great might,*
*To guide mankind, with truth and light.*

*From humble care, a bond was born,*
*Halima's love, a life adorned.*
*Through milk she fed the blessed one,*
*The Prophet's light, like rising sun.*

---

[16] Halima: The foster mother of Prophet Muhammad (PBUH), who cared for him during his early years in the desert, providing him with love and nurturing.

### *The Blessing of Khadija and the Dawn of Prophethood*

*In Mecca's heart, Khadija [17]stood,*
*A woman strong, both kind and good.*
*Her wealth was vast, her fame profound,*
*But in Muhammad, trust she found.*

*She sent him forth, her trade to lead,*
*With honesty, he did succeed.*
*His modest ways, his noble fate,*
*Left Maysarah [18]the servant, amazed.*

*The profits soared, their venture blessed,*
*And Khadija's heart could find no rest.*
*In secret, through a friend's kind word,*
*Her wish to wed the Prophet stirred.*

*Their union bloomed, a love divine,*
*With daughters blessed, a sacred line.*
*Zainab, Ruqayya, and Fatima too,*
*Umm Kulthum's [19]smile, a bond so true.*

*Though sons they lost, in heaven kept,*
*Their hearts remained, in faith adept.*

---

[17] Khadija: The first wife of Prophet Muhammad (PBUH), a successful businesswoman and the first person to embrace Islam, offering unwavering support and faith in him.

[18] Maysarah: The servant of Khadija, who accompanied Prophet Muhammad (PBUH) on a trading journey to Syria and witnessed his honesty and integrity, which led to Khadija proposing marriage to him.

[19] Umm Kulthum: The daughter of Prophet Muhammad (PBUH) and Khadija, known for her piety, wisdom, and strong character. She was one of the Prophet's beloved daughters.

*Khadija's wealth, her every part,*
*She gave to him with all her heart.*

## The Revelation and Khadija's Unwavering Support

*For years in Mecca, he prepared,*
*His wisdom grew, his soul repaired.*
*Until one night in Hira's cave,*
*The revelation that God gave.*

*Upon maturity, the Prophet stood,*
*In visions clear, his soul was good.*
*True dreams he saw, like dawn's first light,*
*A sign of greatness in his sight.*

*On Ramadan's [20] night, the twenty-seventh,*
*In Hira's cave[21], he sought the heavens.*
*Gabriel [22] came with words to share,*
*The first of God's divine affair.*

*"Recite," he said, but Muhammad replied,*
*"I am not a reader," his heart denied.*
*Three times it came, the angel's plea,*
*Till finally, the Prophet did agree.*

---

[20] Ramadan: The ninth month of the Islamic lunar calendar, observed by Muslims worldwide as a time of fasting, prayer, reflection, and community, commemorating the first revelation of the Qur'an to Prophet Muhammad (PBUH).

[21] Hira's Cave: A cave located near Mecca, where Prophet Muhammad (PBUH) received the first revelation of the Qur'an from the angel Gabriel, marking the beginning of his prophethood.

[22] Gabriel: An archangel in Islam, known as Jibril in Arabic, who delivered Allah's revelations to Prophet Muhammad (PBUH) and other prophets, acting as a messenger of divine guidance.

*Sweat upon his brow did shine,*
*A moment etched in sacred time.*
*The first of verses, pure and bright,*
*God's words descending through the night.*

*This meeting grand, the Earth and skies,*
*The messenger from heaven flies.*
*Gabriel's presence, firm and sure,*
*With words of truth forever pure.*

*The Prophet left the cave in haste,*
*To Khadija, he made his case.*
*No friend or kin did he consult,*
*But to his wife, his heart's result.*

*This bond so deep, this trust so strong,*
*In Khadija's arms, he did belong.*
*He told her of the sight he'd seen,*
*Of Gabriel's words and what they mean.*

*Trembling still from revelation's weight,*
*He asked for warmth, for love innate.*
*"Cover me, cover me," he cried,*
*And in her care, his fear subsides.*

*Khadija, wise, with faith so grand,*
*Sought counsel from a learned man.*
*Her cousin, Waraqa[23], a sage of old,*
*Who knew of scriptures once foretold.*

---

[23] Waraqa: The cousin of Khadija and a Christian scholar, who recognized the divine nature of Prophet Muhammad's (PBUH) revelation when he shared his experience in Hira's Cave, affirming his prophethood.

"This is the law," he did proclaim,
"The same to Moses[24], it once came."
A truth so clear, a path so bright,
For Muhammad now, the guiding light.

But Waraqa spoke with heavy heart,
For from his age, he'd soon depart.
"I wish," he said, "to stand beside,
When your people turn you aside."

The Prophet, shocked, could not believe,
His people would his cause deceive.
"But none before have brought this way,
Without a trial, without dismay."

Waraqa, the man with wisdom vast,
Upon hearing the news, he spoke at last:
"If I live to see that day arrive,
I will stand by you, O Muhammad, alive."

"I'll support you with victory grand,"
He vowed to aid with steadfast hand.
But Waraqa's days were numbered few,
And soon he passed, the sky withdrew.

And so it was, the journey started,
The Prophet's mission now imparted.
With Khadija's love and faith so true,
The message spread, the world anew.

---

[24] Moses: A prophet in Islam, known as Musa, revered for leading the Israelites out of Egypt and receiving the Torah, symbolizing faith, courage, and divine guidance.

## The Transition from Secrecy to Proclamation and The First Migration

*In Mecca's bounds, the truth lay sealed,*
*A whispered call, a faith revealed.*
*But soon the word from God on high,*
*Commanded, rise and let it fly!*

*The time had come; no more concealed,*
*The truth proclaimed, the call revealed.*
*With wisdom sharp and strategy clear,*
*The Prophet's voice rang far and near.*

*Within his home, a sacred space,*
*The faithful gathered face to face.*
*Al-Arqam's house [25] became the site,*
*Where hearts were lit with guiding light.*

*The strong and weak, the bold and meek,*
*All came to find the peace they'd seek.*
*Hamza [26] and Umar [27], steadfast, true,*
*Their strength revived the faithful few.*

---

[25] Al-Arqam's House: The secret meeting place for early Muslims in Mecca, where Prophet Muhammad (PBUH) and his followers gathered to pray and discuss Islam during times of persecution.

[26] Hamza: The uncle of Prophet Muhammad (PBUH) and a prominent early supporter of Islam, known for his bravery and strength. He became a martyr in the Battle of Uhud, earning the title "Lion of Allah."

[27] Umar: The second caliph of Islam, known for his strong leadership, justice, and contributions to the expansion of the Islamic empire. Initially an opponent of Islam, he later became one of its most steadfast supporters.

*But with the call, a storm arose,*
*The Quraysh defied and turned to foes.*
*With scorn and harm, they sought to break,*
*The mission stirred for truth's own sake.*

*The first migration then took flight,*
*To Abyssinia's [28]haven bright.*
*A just king ruled that peaceful land,*
*With open heart and guiding hand.*

*Seventy souls left home behind,*
*In search of peace they longed to find.*
*By God's own grace, they found their stay,*
*Safe and sound, from fear's dismay.*

*From whispers soft to bold acclaim,*
*The Prophet spread the sacred name.*
*Through trials fierce and journeys vast,*
*His call to faith would ever last.*

*In sorrow's shadow, the Prophet stood,*
*Grief upon grief, misunderstood.*
*Khadijah's love, his steady guide,*
*And Abu Talib, now not by his side.*

*With their loss, the trials grew,*
*A year of sorrow, harsh and true.*
*Yet from the depths, a gift was sent,*
*A night divine, by heaven meant.*

---

[28] Abyssinia: An ancient kingdom located in the Horn of Africa, known today as Ethiopia. It is significant in Islamic history for providing refuge to the early Muslims who fled persecution in Mecca and sought asylum there under the Christian king, Negus.

## The Journey Beyond Earthly Bounds: Isra' and Mi'raj[29]

*The night of Isra', a tale divine,*
*When Prophet Muhammad crossed the line.*
*To Al-Aqsa Mosque [30]he was swiftly taken,*
*A journey no soul could have mistaken.*

*On the 27th of Rajab[31], as it's almost told,*
*Though dates may shift as time unfolds.*
*Gabriel came, in form so bright,*
*To guide the Prophet through the night.*

*With Buraq[32], the creature swift and strong,*
*The Prophet traveled, the night not long.*
*Its speed so great, its hoofs did soar,*
*To where the eye could see no more.*

*From Sacred Mosque to Al-Aqsa's land,*
*The Prophet stood, by God's command.*

---

[29] Isra' and Mi'raj: The miraculous night journey and ascension of Prophet Muhammad (PBUH), during which he traveled from Mecca to Jerusalem and then ascended to the heavens, receiving guidance and blessings from Allah.

[30] Al-Aqsa Mosque: A revered mosque in Jerusalem, the third holiest site in Islam, where Prophet Muhammad (PBUH) is believed to have ascended to the heavens during the Mi'raj.

[31] Rajab: The seventh month of the Islamic lunar calendar, considered one of the four sacred months in which fighting is prohibited, and a time of reflection and spiritual growth for Muslims.

[32] Buraq: A mystical creature in Islamic tradition, described as a steed larger than a donkey but smaller than a mule, which carried Prophet Muhammad (PBUH) during his night journey (Isra') from Mecca to Jerusalem.

*He prayed with prophets, a sacred scene,*
*Before ascending through realms unseen.*

*Mi'raj; through the heavens, he made his way,*
*Meeting prophets in bright array.*
*Abraham, Moses, Idris, and more,*
*In each heaven, wisdom they bore.*

*In the Seventh Heaven, a moment grand,*
*God gave the prayer, His direct command.*
*Not on earth, but high above,*
*The prayer was gifted, a sign of love.*

*The skeptics scoffed in Mecca's streets,*
*"How could he make such daring feats?"*
*"Months we take by camel's pace,*
*Yet he claims a journey at lightning's grace?"*

*To Abu Bakr [33]they quickly ran,*
*Mocking the Prophet's faithful man.*
*"Did you hear what Muhammad said?*
*That in one night, he traveled ahead?"*

*Abu Bakr's answer, calm and clear,*
*"I believe what he brings from heaven near.*
*If I trust in news from realms so high,*
*Why doubt his journey through the sky?"*

*From that day on, his title came,*
*Al-Siddiq, truthful in name.*

---

[33] Abu Bakr: The closest companion and the first caliph of Islam after the death of Prophet Muhammad (PBUH). Known for his wisdom, piety, and unwavering support, he played a key role in the early spread of Islam.

*A mark of faith so pure and strong,*
*That in history's tale, it would belong.*

*The Isra', a moment rare and grand,*
*A night of wonders from God's hand.*
*Yet Mecca's trials did not cease,*
*The Prophet sought a place of peace.*

*Through harm and hardship, he did strive,*
*Looking for a way to survive.*
*The first and second Aqaba's pact,*
*With people of Medina[34], a solemn act.*

*He sought a land where faith could grow,*
*Where safety and peace would overflow.*
*A place to build the state of Islam,*
*Away from Mecca's growing harm.*

*Thus began the journey anew,*
*Toward Medina, a vision true.*
*A city where Islam would bloom,*
*And from its heart, the world consume.*

---

[34] Medina: The second holiest city in Islam, where Prophet Muhammad (PBUH) migrated to from Mecca, establishing the first Islamic state and community, and where he is buried.

## *The Prophet's Sacred Flight to Medina*

*In the quiet night, as Mecca slept,
The Prophet, with trust in his heart, kept.
Not fleeing in fear, but with purpose bright,
He planned each step in the cloak of night.*

*Most companions had gone ahead,
Yet he stayed behind, no trace of dread.
Ali[35], in his bed, as the Prophet's shield,
Trusts returned, no debts concealed.*

*The Quraysh gathered, swords held tight,
Seeking his life in the dead of night.
But at the cave, where hope seemed slim,
God stood firm with Abu Bakr and him.*

*If they looked down, they'd surely see,
Yet with God beside us, we're truly free.
Danger loomed, but faith shone clear,
Their safety sealed, no cause for fear.*

*In the desert came Suraqa's [36]ride,
For camels promised, he chased with pride.*

---

[35] Ali: The cousin and son-in-law of Prophet Muhammad (PBUH), the fourth caliph of Islam, known for his wisdom, bravery, and devotion. He is revered for his leadership and role in early Islamic history.

[36] Suraqa: A Bedouin who initially pursued Prophet Muhammad (PBUH) during his migration to Medina with the intention of capturing him, but later embraced Islam after witnessing the Prophet's righteousness and the fulfillment of a prophecy about Suraqa's eventual wealth.

*But his horse sank low in the shifting sand,*
*As the Prophet's promise stayed God's command.*

*"A crown awaits you, not here today,*
*But in Persia's land, where kings once lay."*
*With these words, Suraqa's heart found peace,*
*And he rode away, letting pursuit cease.*

*Arriving in Medina, the Prophet stood tall,*
*His mission divine, a beacon for all.*

## The Shift of Sacred Prayer

When the Prophet arrived in Medina's land,
His camel stopped at God's command.
In that place, a mosque arose,
A symbol of faith where piety flows.

Quba' Mosque[37], the first of its kind,
Built on devotion, with peace in mind.
A house of worship, pure and bright,
A beacon born from the Prophet's light.

For months, he prayed towards Jerusalem's skies,
And in Medina, the Jews would criticize.
"How could Muhammad claim Abraham's way,
Yet to our qibla, his prayers he'd sway?"

But God knew the burden within his heart,
The Prophet would gaze at the stars, apart.
Until the night of Shaban's [38] grace,
When the Lord revealed a new sacred place.

"Turn your face towards Mecca's ground,
The Sacred Mosque[39], where truth is found."

---

[37] Quba' Mosque: The first mosque built in Islam, located near Medina. It was established by Prophet Muhammad (PBUH) and his companions during their migration (Hijrah) and holds great significance for its early role in the Muslim community.

[38] Shaban: The eighth month of the Islamic lunar calendar, a time of preparation for Ramadan. It is known for the practice of fasting and acts of charity, and for the night of the 15th of Shaban, which is considered a blessed night in some Islamic traditions.

[39] The Sacred Mosque (Al-Masjid al-Haram): The holiest mosque in Islam, located in Mecca, Saudi Arabia.

*From that day forth, the qibla changed,*
*As faith and guidance were rearranged.*

*With this shift, a sign so grand,*
*The unity of faith spread across the land.*
*And the mosque of Quba stood proud and tall,*
*As Islam's foundation, welcoming all.*

## Badr[40]: The Day of Triumph and Faith

In Ramadan's sacred, fasting hour,
The Battle of Badr revealed God's power.
A clash unsought, but by fate aligned,
The Quraysh's doom by God's design.

Three hundred men, with faith so deep,
While Quraysh marched in forceful sweep.
One thousand strong, their banners high,
Yet truth would pierce their boastful lie.

Abu Sufyan's [41] caravan veered,
Yet Quraysh advanced, their hearts steered by fear.
Arrogance drove them into war,
Not knowing what lay yet in store.

The Prophet, wise, made his stand,
With wells dug deep in desert sand.
His men prepared with thoughtful care,
Trusting God in this affair.

The angels came to aid the fight,
Descending swift in purest light.

---

[40] Badr: A pivotal battle in Islamic history, fought in 624 CE between the early Muslims of Medina and the Quraysh of Mecca. It is celebrated for the divine assistance granted to the Muslims, leading to a decisive victory.
[41] Abu Sufyan: A prominent leader of the Quraysh tribe and a fierce opponent of Islam during the early years. He later embraced Islam after the conquest of Mecca, playing a key role in the expansion of the Islamic community.

*With swords unseen, they struck the foe,*
*As terror seized their hearts below.*

*Seventy lost, their leaders slain,*
*Quraysh now bore defeat's harsh stain.*
*Their armor heavy, their courage thinned,*
*As God's own army surged to win.*

*Spoils left in the desert wide,*
*And prisoners bound in chains with pride.*
*The Muslims rose with newfound might,*
*Their banner shining in the night.*

*This was the day that changed the tale,*
*When faith and courage did prevail.*
*The tribes now knew the Prophet's call,*
*For God's own hand had guided all.*

## *Uhud's [42]Turning Tide: A Lesson of Obedience*

*In Shawwal's [43]month, the Quraysh sought,*
*Revenge for Badr, their pride distraught.*
*Three thousand strong, with hearts of steel,*
*They marched to fight, their fate concealed.*

*The Prophet heard their battle cry,*
*With counsel sought, his men stood by.*
*Young voices called, "Let's fight outside!"*
*With youthful zeal, they would not hide.*

*Mount Uhud stood, a mighty shield,*
*Behind its rocks, their backs concealed.*
*"Fifty archers," the Prophet decreed,*
*"Guard the heights; fulfill this need.*
*Hold your ground, let none defy,*
*Watch the rear, and guard the sky."*

*Victory gleamed for those who fought,*
*The Quraysh scattered, hope seemed naught.*
*But spoils below, a tempting sight,*
*Led archers down, abandoning height.*

---

[42] Uhud: The site of the Battle of Uhud, fought in 625 CE between the early Muslims of Medina and the Quraysh of Mecca. Although the Muslims initially gained the upper hand, the battle turned in favor of the Quraysh due to a strategic error, leading to heavy casualties, including the martyrdom of Prophet Muhammad's (PBUH) uncle, Hamza.

[43] Shawwal: The tenth month of the Islamic lunar calendar, known for the celebration of Eid al-Fitr at its beginning, marking the end of Ramadan. It is also significant for fasting six additional days, which is considered highly rewarding in Islam.

*Disobedience came with a heavy price,*
*Khalid [44]returned, his strike precise.*
*The lines were broken, chaos reigned,*
*A costly lesson, sharp and pained.*

*The beloved trapped, his men now few,*

*Yet courage rose in hearts so true.*
*His blood was shed, let the heavens cry,*
*Yet honor shone as martyrs died.*

*Disobedience turned the day,*
*From triumph's grasp to loss's sway.*
*Uhud taught what all must see,*
*In following trust, we find victory.*

*Today we feel the echoes still,*
*When orders lost, our fates stand still.*
*For every field where we have failed,*
*The lesson of Uhud prevail.*

---

[44] Khalid: Khalid ibn al-Walid, known as "The Sword of Allah," was a renowned general in early Islamic history, celebrated for his military genius and leadership in key battles, including the Battle of Uhud and the Battle of Yarmouk. He initially opposed Islam but later became one of its most ardent supporters and a key figure in its expansion.

## *The Winds of Defeat: The Battle of the Trench*

*A storm was brewing across the land,*
*Quraysh and tribes, united they stand.*
*With Ghatafan and Bani Salim's [45]might,*
*They sought to crush Islam's light.*

*Tribes united, ten thousand strong,*
*A mighty force, it wouldn't be long.*
*But the Prophet, wise and full of grace,*
*Sought counsel in this pressing case.*

*Salman [46]spoke, with wisdom clear,*
*"In Persia, trenches hold foes in fear."*
*The Prophet smiled and took this plan,*
*A trench was dug by every man.*

*The tribes arrived, but stood dismayed,*
*Unfamiliar with this wall displayed.*
*They could not pass, their strength was drained,*
*Their hopes of conquest now remained.*

---

[45] Ghatafan and Bani Salim: A powerful Arab tribe that opposed the early Muslim community, particularly during the Battle of the Confederates (Ahzab) in 627 CE, when they allied with the Quraysh to besiege Medina. However, the siege ended in failure, and the Ghatafan tribe later made peace with the Muslims.

[46] Salman: Salman al-Farsi, a companion of Prophet Muhammad (PBUH), originally from Persia. He is known for his search for truth, which led him to Islam, and his key role in suggesting the digging of a trench during the Battle of the Confederates (Ahzab), a strategy that helped protect Medina from the attacking forces.

*Then came a wind, fierce and strong,*
*It tore through camps and righted wrongs.*
*God's command swept through the night,*
*The enemies fled, consumed by fright.*

*With Quraysh gone, the Prophet turned,*
*To Banu Quraydha[47], who had spurned.*
*A pact they broke, betrayal clear,*
*The Prophet judged, their fate severe.*

*To Banu Lihyan [48]the Muslims did ride,*
*But the enemy fled and chose to hide.*

*The Battle of the Trench was won,*
*By faith and wind, not sword or gun.*
*A tale of trust, of strength unseen,*
*In God's command, victory is seen.*

---

[47] Banu Quraydha: A Jewish tribe in Medina that broke their pact with the Muslims during the Battle of the Confederates (Ahzab) in 627 CE, leading to their defeat and subsequent punishment by the Muslim community.

[48] Banu Lihyan: A nomadic Arab tribe that opposed the early Muslims. They played a role in the Battle of Uhud by allying with the Quraysh and other groups against the Muslims but were later subdued by the Muslim forces.

## The Treaty of Hudaybiyyah[49]: A Tale of Truce and Betrayal

In Hudaybiyyah, a truce was found,
A peace, though fragile, in sacred ground.
The Prophet came with Umrah in sight,
But Quraysh denied him the holy right.

"By God, he won't enter!" Quraysh declared,
Though customs of peace had long been shared.
Yet messengers came, and terms were set,
A treaty signed, though hearts still fret.

For ten long years, the swords would sleep,
But alliances ran dark and deep.
Whoever wished, could choose their side,
With Quraysh or Muhammad, their tribes allied.

Yet one condition, harsh and rare,
If one fled to Quraysh, they'd find their care.
But should one seek refuge, leaving their kin,
The Prophet would send them back within.

Omar[50], troubled, could not believe,
That in their faith, they'd still concede.

---

[49] Hudaybiyyah: The site of a pivotal treaty in 628 CE between Prophet Muhammad (PBUH) and the Quraysh of Mecca. Known as the Treaty of Hudaybiyyah, it was a peace agreement that allowed Muslims to perform the pilgrimage to Mecca the following year and played a crucial role in the spread of Islam.
[50] Omar: Omar ibn al-Khattab, the second caliph of Islam

*But patience, the Prophet firmly taught,*
*In God's plan, a victory sought.*

*Khaybar's [51] strongholds fell one by one,*
*Their power dimmed by the light of Islam's sun.*
*At Mu'tah's [52] field, the banners stood tall,*
*Though Zayd and others answered the call.*

*Two tribes arose, in ancient feud,*
*Banu Khuza'ah [53] sought a bond renewed.*
*But Quraysh, in secret, fueled the flame,*
*And Banu Bakr [54] attacked in shame.*

---

[51] Khaybar: A fortress town in Arabia, home to Jewish tribes, which was the site of a significant battle in 629 CE. The Muslim forces, led by Prophet Muhammad (PBUH), defeated the defending Jewish tribes of Khaybar, resulting in the Muslims gaining control of the area and its resources. The victory strengthened the Islamic community and marked an important moment in the early expansion of Islam.

[52] Mu'tah: The site of the Battle of Mu'tah in 629 CE, fought between the Muslim forces and the Byzantine Empire's allies, the Ghassanid Arabs. Despite being vastly outnumbered, the Muslims, led by Zayd ibn Haritha, showed remarkable bravery. The battle ended with the martyrdom of the Muslim commanders, and Khalid ibn al-Walid took command, ensuring a strategic withdrawal. The battle is significant for demonstrating the courage and resilience of the early Muslim army.

[53] Banu Khuza'ah: A prominent Arab tribe in the pre-Islamic period that became allies of the Prophet Muhammad (PBUH) after their support during the conquest of Mecca. They played a crucial role in the peaceful entry of the Muslims into Mecca and were instrumental in the negotiations leading to the Treaty of Hudaybiyyah.

[54] Banu Bakr: An Arab tribe that, along with the Quraysh, violated the Treaty of Hudaybiyyah by attacking the Banu Khuza'ah tribe, who were allies of the Muslims. This breach of the treaty led to the eventual conquest of Mecca in 630 CE by the Muslims, as the Quraysh were held accountable for their allies' actions.

*The massacre broke the treaty's seal,*
*Betrayal clear, the wound revealed.*
*The truce was shattered, the die was cast,*
*And war approached, its shadow vast.*

*The Prophet's allies, in desperate plea,*
*Called for justice, called to be free.*
*Quraysh had broken their sacred vow,*
*And the time for peace was over now.*

## *The Conquest of Mecca*

*In Ramadan's glow, beneath its light,
Ten thousand marched, prepared for the fight.
The Prophet led, with peace in hand,
To conquer Mecca, the holy land.*

*The Quraysh who once mocked his name,
Now wondered, would he seek the same?
But mercy spoke through his decree:
"No blame is yours; you all are free."*

*"Who enters the mosque, or Abu Sufyan's door,
Shall be safe and spared from war."
No race to cleanse, no blood to spill,
His goal was unity, peace, and goodwill.*

*The city that once had cause him pain,
Now witnessed his victory, clear and plain.
Bilal [55] called out from atop the Kaaba's height,
Proclaiming God's Oneness with all his might.*

*The idols fell[56], the truth stood tall,
The call to prayer echoed through it all.*

---

[55] Bilal: Bilal ibn Rabah, one of the most revered companions of Prophet Muhammad (PBUH), was the first African and one of the earliest converts to Islam. Known for his unwavering faith and resilience, he became the first muezzin (caller to prayer) in Islam. His iconic voice called the believers to prayer, symbolizing equality and justice in the nascent Muslim community.

[56] The idols fell: The statues that had been placed around and inside the Kaaba were destroyed, symbolizing the end of idolatry and the establishment of monotheism in the holy sanctuary. This marked a significant moment in the spread of Islam.

*Mecca was cleansed, hearts made pure,*
*A victory for all of humanity, forever sure.*

*This wasn't just a conquest won,*
*But a dawn of peace, with faith begun.*
*A clear victory, as God had said,*
*For all the living, and the honored dead.*

## *The Prophet's Farewell: A Final Call*

*After Mecca's conquest bright,*
*The Prophet stood in radiant light.*
*He made his Hajj[57], the one farewell,*
*To a nation that in droves would swell.*

*In the tenth year, his journey began,*
*With peace, he led both woman and man.*
*To the Sacred House, they all did tread,*
*As his final words of wisdom spread.*

*In the plains of Arafat's [58]embrace,*
*The Prophet stood with shining grace.*
*A final sermon, clear and bright,*
*A call to justice, truth, and light.*

*"O People, lend your ears to me,*
*For this may be the last you see."*
*Your blood, your wealth, your honor dear,*
*Are sacred as this day stands clear."*

---

[57] Hajj: The annual pilgrimage to Mecca, one of the Five Pillars of Islam, obligatory for Muslims who are physically and financially able to undertake it. Hajj involves a series of rituals performed over several days, including the Tawaf (circumambulating the Kaaba), standing at Arafat, and symbolic acts such as the stoning of the pillars. It is a profound spiritual journey that symbolizes unity, equality, and submission to Allah.

[58] Arafat: A plain near Mecca, significant in Islam for being the site of the annual standing (Wuquf) during Hajj, where pilgrims gather on the 9th of Dhu al-Hijjah. It is a day of prayer, reflection, and seeking forgiveness from Allah. The event marks a key part of Hajj and is considered a day of mercy and salvation.

*He praised the One, the Lord Most High,*
*Creator of earth, sea, and sky.*
*"Our Lord is One, the Great; the True,*
*In piety alone lies worth in you.*

*"No Arab above a non-Arab stand,*
*Nor black nor white claims higher lands.*
*In deeds and faith, our worth is found,*
*In this, equality shall abound."*

*Then he spoke of life's sacred trust,*
*Of property and honor, just.*
*"Like Mecca, this day, this month revered,*
*So too, all life must be endeared.*

*Return what's owed, let no harm fall,*
*For justice must be shared by all."*

*Pre-Islamic ways, he cast aside,*
*With usury, vengeance denied.*
*"All debts of ignorance I free,*
*The first I end from kin, you see."*

*The rights of women, he did proclaim,*
*"Fear Allah, treat them the same.*
*They're partners, not mere hands to use,*
*With kindness, honor them, don't abuse."*

*He called to worship, five times a day,*
*Ramadan's fast, Zakat [59] to pay.*

---

[59] Zakat: One of the Five Pillars of Islam, Zakat is a form of obligatory charity aimed at redistributing wealth to those in need. It requires Muslims to give a portion (usually 2.5%) of their accumulated wealth and assets annually to the poor and needy, fostering social welfare and reducing inequality.

*And for the strong who could afford,*
*To journey forth and praise the Lord.*

*"All Muslims are as brothers here,*
*No wealth is right that's claimed by fear.*
*Only with joy should gifts be shared,*
*In brotherhood, let hearts be paired."*

*A warning sharp he then did state,*
*"Beware of Satan, his subtle bait.*
*He won't lead you in large deceit,*
*But in small sins, he'll seek defeat."*

*The Qur'an and Sunnah[60], bright as light,*
*He left as guidance in the night.*
*"Hold fast to these, and you'll not stray,*
*Let them guide your life each day."*

*And then, with gravity profound,*
*He spoke of Judgment's holy ground.*
*"O People, know, before Allah's throne,*
*Your deeds will stand, each one is shown."*

*His voice then rose, his eyes alight,*
*"Have I conveyed the message right?"*
*The crowd agreed, their hands did raise,*
*"O Allah, witness their praise!"*

*"Let all who hear, convey this truth,*
*To those afar, and to the youth.*

---

[60] Sunnah: The practices, actions, and sayings of Prophet Muhammad (PBUH), which serve as a model for Muslims to follow in their daily lives. The Sunnah, along with the Qur'an, forms the primary source of Islamic law and guidance, providing a practical interpretation of the teachings of Islam.

*For this, the message clear and grand,*
*Must spread across both sea and land."*

His best companion, Abou Bakr, cried,
For he knew the end was nigh.
He left us with a call so deep,
A faith to hold, a trust to keep.

Thus, in the farewell of the last,
A message timeless, unsurpassed.
In every word, a truth profound,
The path to peace is all around.

Then back to Medina, he returned,
With love and peace, the nation yearned.
For a few more months, he lived his grace,
Before meeting his Lord, in a heavenly place.

## *Mothers of the Believers*
## *(Ummahat al-Mu'minin[61])*

*Behold the sun, whose light we trace,*
*Encircled by stars of timeless grace.*
*Eleven wives in the heavens' expanse,*
*Mothers of the believers, in a sacred stance.*

***Khadijah**, first and brightest star,*
*Who stood with faith through trials afar.*
*Her wealth, her heart, her endless care,*
*A legacy of love, beyond compare.*

*Then **Sawda**[62], steady, strong, and kind,*
*A refuge for the Prophet's mind.*
*Her humor brightened the darkest night,*
*Her loyalty firm, a guiding light.*

***Aisha**, young, with wisdom vast,*
*A scholar whose words forever last.*
*Through her we learn the Prophet's way,*
*A treasure of hadith, still bright today.*

---

[61] Ummahat al-Mu'minin: Translated as "Mothers of the Believers," this term refers to the wives of Prophet Muhammad (PBUH). They hold a special status in Islam, respected for their roles in preserving and transmitting the teachings of Islam. Their lives and actions serve as models of piety and virtue for Muslims.

[62] Sawda: Arabic name; as other names in this poem; Sawda bint Zam'a was one of the wives of Prophet Muhammad (PBUH) known for her kindness and devotion. She was the second woman to marry the Prophet after Khadijah's death. Sawda is particularly remembered for her generosity and her support of the Prophet during difficult times. She was also known for her strong faith and role in early Islamic history.

***Hafsa***, *keeper of Qur'anic lines,*
*A guardian of the sacred signs.*
*Her steadfast heart, her noble soul,*
*Preserved the Book that makes us whole.*

***Zaynab of Khuzayma***, *tender and pure,*
*Her charity lives, her legacy sure.*
*Though brief her time, her love was wide,*
*A mother to the poor, in whom hope abides.*

***Umm Salama***, *wise and true,*
*With counsel deep, she always knew.*
*A pillar of strength in times of despair,*
*Her wisdom taught us to persevere.*

***Zaynab bint Jahsh***, *of noble creed,*
*Who followed faith where it would lead.*
*Her marriage broke the chains of old,*
*A story of courage, divinely told.*

***Juwayriya***, *with grace profound,*
*Her union brought peace all around.*
*A tribe united, hearts made whole,*
*Through her, we learn diplomacy's role.*

***Umm Habiba***, *steadfast and brave,*
*Through trials, her faith she gave.*
*From distant lands, her loyalty shone,*
*Her heart forever the Prophet's own.*

***Safiyyah***, *star of a humbled past,*
*Whose dignity rose and love held fast.*
*Through her, we see how hearts transform,*
*A union of peace after the storm.*

*And last,* **Maymunah**, *purest name,*
*The final star in this radiant frame.*
*Her piety vast, her faith complete,*
*A model of grace, in every feat.*

*These mothers of believers, divine and wise,*
*Reflect the Prophet's light in their skies.*
*Through them we learn, through them we see,*
*The depth of love and humanity.*

## *Jewels of the Prophet's Line*

*Around the Prophet, a sacred glow,*
*His children, jewels, whose virtues show.*
*Each a testament, pure and bright,*
*Reflecting his love, his guiding light.*

***Qasim**[63], firstborn, a shining flame,*
*Who graced the Prophet with his name.*
*Though brief his time, his light remains,*
*A link to hope through joys and pains.*

***Zainab**, eldest, gentle and true,*
*With steadfast faith, her spirit grew.*
*Through trials faced with courage rare,*
*A mother's heart, beyond compare.*

***Ruqayyah**, a star so fair,*
*Whose patience adorned her with heavenly flair.*
*Through trials she walked, her faith held fast,*
*A beacon of strength in times that passed.*

***Umm Kulthum**, serene, steadfast,*
*A jewel of grace that time couldn't outlast.*
*Her loyalty firm, her love complete,*
*A daughter's devotion, gentle and sweet.*

---

[63] Qasim: Arabic name, same as other names mentioned in this poem; Qasim ibn Muhammad was the first son of Prophet Muhammad (PBUH) and his first wife, Khadijah. Although he died in infancy, Qasim holds a special place in Islamic history as one of the Prophet's children. His early death deeply affected the Prophet, but he remains a symbol of the family of the Prophet in Islamic tradition.

***Fatimah***, *the radiant pearl,*
*The Prophet's heart, his cherished girl.*
*With Ali, she shone as a guiding light,*
*A legacy blooming in her children's sight.*

***Abdullah***, *the pure and young,*
*Whose life, though brief, is forever sung.*
*A reminder of love, so tender and deep,*
*In the Prophet's prayers, his soul shall keep.*

***Ibrahim***, *last of the line,*
*Born in Medina, a joy divine.*
*Though his time was short, his memory stays,*
*A promise of peace in eternal days.*

*These sons and daughters, gifts from above,*
*Reflections of the Prophet's boundless love.*
*Through them, his legacy flows like a stream,*
*A living proof of the blessed dream.*

*We've been commanded to cherish their name,*
*To honor their lives and their noble claim.*
*In loving them, our faith takes flight,*
*A bond to the Prophet, shining bright.*

## The Ashraf of Creation's Names

*Beloved one, let us proclaim,*
*The radiant glow of each blessed name.*
*The Ashraf of Creation, shining bright,*
*Each name a flame, a guiding light.*

*From the lips of those who call You near,*
*A song of love, so pure, so clear.*

*O Chosen One, Al-Mustafa[64], so bright,*
*You shine as Noor, a guiding light.*
*Muhammad, praised in heaven's hymn,*
*Ahmad, where all praises begin.*

*Al-Amin, the Trustworthy, true,*
*Al-Sadiq, the Honest, through and through.*
*Rahmatun lil-Alamin, mercy vast,*
*A refuge for hearts, a love that will last.*

*Al-Nabi, the Prophet, ever near,*
*Al-Rasul, the Messenger, held dear.*
*Al-Mahi, who erases disbelief's trace,*
*Al-Hashir, whom we all gather in grace.*

*The Seal of Prophets, the last divine,*
*Through him, Allah's truths align.*

---

[64] Al-Mustafa: An Arabic title; like other titles in this poem; meaning "The Chosen One," often used to refer to Prophet Muhammad (PBUH). It highlights his distinguished status as the final messenger and prophet chosen by Allah to deliver the message of Islam to humanity. The title signifies his unique role and exemplary character in guiding Muslims to the truth.

Al-Muddathir, the Cloaked, serene,
Al-Muzammil, the Wrapped, unseen.

Al-Bashir, bearer of glad news,
Al-Nadhir, who warns and imbues.
Siraj Munir, a radiant flame,
Al-Hadi, the Guide, who calls our name.

The Beloved of Allah, Habib so dear,
Imam al-Mursalin, to lead without fear.
Sayyid al-Mursalin, noble and great,
Ashraf al-khalq, in every state.

Al-Adl, the Just, in balance he stands,
Rauf and Rahim, with compassionate hands.
Nabiy al-Rahma, Mercy's delight,
Nabiy al-Tawba, through forgiveness' light.

Al-Tahir, the Pure, in heart and soul,
Al-Mutawakkil, trusting Allah whole.
Al-Mansur, in victory crowned,
Ya Rasool Allah, where blessings abound.

Ya Nabi Allah, heaven's delight,
Al-Munir, in the darkest night.
Al-Kareem, Generous, tender and kind,
Through his names, God's mercy we find.

Each name a treasure, a timeless embrace,
A mirror of Allah's boundless grace.
Muhammad, Ahmad, by any name,
The mercy for all, forever the same.

## *When the Light Fades*

*Beneath a sky so still, so gray,*
*The Prophet, our guide, began to sway.*
*In fever's grip, his breath grew slow,*
*And hearts around him sank in woe.*

*Aisha held him, her touch so light,*
*He glanced at the Siwak[65], a silent sight.*
*She knew his wish, without a word,*
*She softened it, as love stirred.*

*Their last exchange, a final act,*
*The man who brought them light intact.*
*His wives, with tear-streaked faces bowed,*
*For death had come, its call was loud.*

*In that room, where silence fell,*
*The air grew thick with a heavy spell.*
*The angels whispered, hovering near,*
*For the end of his time was now so clear.*

*His eyes, once bright, began to close,*
*The world outside in sorrow froze.*
*With trembling lips, he called to say,*
*"The Highest Companion is my way."*

---

[65] Siwak: A teeth-cleaning tool made from the twigs of the Salvadora persica tree, used traditionally in many Muslim cultures. It is highly recommended in Islam for maintaining oral hygiene, as Prophet Muhammad (PBUH) is known to have used it regularly. The siwak is valued for its natural cleansing properties and its role in Sunnah practices.

*A gasp escaped, a life's last word,*
*And in the stillness, nothing stirred.*
*Umar, fierce and strong, could not believe,*
*Grief so raw, he could hardly breathe.*

*"No!" he cried, his sword unsheathed,*
*"Who claims his death, I'll strike beneath!"*
*Ali fell, unable to stand,*
*Uthman's[66] palms clasped, trembling hand.*

*Oh, the light, it dimmed, it died,*
*Medina's glow, the hope, the pride.*
*The streets that once with laughter rang,*
*Now echoed only sorrow's pang.*

*"Where are you now?" they begged the skies,*
*For in his loss, the world denies.*
*Tears fell as they buried him low,*
*The sun itself seemed not to glow.*

*But Abu Bakr, voice so clear,*
*Through the sobs that filled the air,*
*Stood firm, his heart a shield of steel,*
*And spoke the words that made them kneel:*

*"Whoever worshipped Muhammad, know,*
*He's gone, he's passed, his light's let go.*

---

[66] Uthman's: Refers to Uthman ibn Affan, the third caliph of the Islamic community, known for his significant contributions to the preservation and compilation of the Qur'an. Uthman ordered the collection of the Qur'an into a single, standardized text, which was then distributed across the Islamic empire. His reign is also marked by expansion and some internal dissent, leading to his eventual martyrdom.

*But those who worship God, take heed,*
*For He lives on, your only need."*

*The Companions wept, a flood of pain,*
*For they would never see him again.*
*Yet in their hearts, he lived, he stayed,*
*A Prophet's love could never fade.*

*His soul ascended, pure and bright,*
*And left them with eternal light.*
*Oh, reader, feel the ache, the loss,*
*For the world had known the greatest cost.*

*But as you cry, remember this;*
*His legacy, our lasting bliss.*
*Though he is gone, his path remains,*
*In every heart, his love sustains.*

*The Ashrafiya Hymn*                *Dr. Ashi Ezz*

## *Muhammad: The Seal of The Prophets.*

*In the time when Muhammad graced the earth,*
*No bond between sky and ground held greater worth.*
*Sixty-three years, divinely blessed,*
*Twenty-three of them, the sacred call addressed.*

*Three years in whispers, a truth concealed,*
*When heaven's light on earth was first revealed.*
*God's love adorned the dearest of mankind,*
*In whom the hearts and souls of all aligned.*

*He spoke of prophets, guiding lights of old,*
*Who built the house of truth with hands so bold.*
*Each laid a brick, each played their part,*
*Their work, a testament of faith and heart.*

*Yet one last brick remained to grace the frame,*
*A void that called for the finest name.*
*"How perfect this house," the people cried,*
*"But one more stone must yet abide."*

*Muhammad, peace upon his soul,*
*Was sent to make the house whole.*
*Like the Black Stone in the sacred space,*
*He sealed the house with heaven's grace.*

*The finest brick, the crown, the best,*
*The last, completing all the rest.*
*God saved the brightest for the final line,*
*A Messenger pure, the seal divine.*

*In form, in purpose, in light so clear,*
*He stood, the final Prophet here.*
*God built this house with wisdom bright,*
*And crowned it with Muhammad, the endless light.*

# Section 2: The Light of His Virtues

## *A Man of Virtue Even in His Youth*

In youth, no recklessness was ever shown,
No shameful act, no sin to call his own.
He walked a path of honor, pure and bright,
While others strayed, he stood in truth's own light.

The people bowed to idols, false and vain,
In rites of ignorance, they sought to gain.
They whistled, blew, and circled 'round the stone,
But he, the Prophet, stood apart, alone.

In pre-Islamic times, when men were lost,
Their deeds of shame, their souls they freely tossed.
They bared themselves in public, with no care,
Yet he, in modesty, did not compare.

No idol did he serve, no falsehood praised,
His heart was pure, untouched by errant ways.
While others clothed in darkness sought to sin,
He stayed the course, his soul remained within.

For even then, the signs were clear and bright,
A man of virtue, walking in the light.
No wrong had touched him, even in his youth,
For he was chosen, set apart for truth.

Thus, from the start, his purity was known,
A proof of what his noble soul had shown.
The Prophet, may God bless and grant him peace,
Was sent to guide, and bring the world release.

*The Ashrafiya Hymn*      *Dr. Ashi Ezz*

## *The Angelic Shadows*

*He walked beneath the heavens, angels near,*
*A cloud-like shade that followed, soft and clear.*
*Each soul who saw him felt a love so deep,*
*From Romans far to Levant's lands, they'd keep.*

*His uncle, Abu Talib, held him tight,*
*When Abdul Muttalib [67] passed to the night.*
*With love so fierce, he could not part his way,*
*And so they traveled north, where merchants lay.*

*To Busra [68] in the Levant lands they came,*
*And there a wiseman, called Bahira [69] by name,*
*Did honor them with welcome rare and bright,*
*For in his eyes, a future shone with light.*

*He saw in Muhammad the signs of grace,*
*The final Prophet, holder of God's place.*
*"Return him home," the wise seer did implore,*
*"I am worried about him from the Jews maybe more.*

---

[67] Abdul Muttalib: The grandfather of Prophet Muhammad (PBUH) and a respected leader of the Quraysh tribe in Mecca. He played a pivotal role in protecting the Kaaba and in maintaining the tribe's status in Meccan society. Abdul Muttalib is best known for his role in the incident of the Year of the Elephant, when he was a key figure in defending Mecca from the Abyssinian invasion. He is also remembered for his strong faith and leadership.

[68] Busra: A historical city located in present-day Syria, known for its significance in early Islamic history.

[69] Bahira: A Christian priest with expertise in ancient texts who recognized the young Prophet Muhammad (PBUH) as the future prophet during a caravan journey to Busra.

*For they will seek to harm this sacred soul,*
*Whose truth will come to light and make him whole."*
*So Abu Talib, in care and love's embrace,*
*Brought back the Prophet to a safer place.*

*Yet angels watched him, guarding from the skies,*
*And even then, the light of truth would rise.*
*For he, the chosen, was known far and wide,*
*A mercy sent, with heaven by his side.*

*The wiseman foretold what time itself would show,*
*That he, Muhammad, was the one to know.*
*A prophet of the end, a guide so true,*
*Whose love and mercy every heart would woo.*

## His Worth, His Honesty, So Pure and Clear

*At twenty-five, his noble heart was pure,*
*A man of honor, steadfast and secure.*
*Khadija, blessed with wealth and lion's pride,*
*Sent forth her wish to stand by his side.*

*She hailed from noble lineage, divine,*
*A house of wealth, where dignity did shine.*
*Her kin and his were bound by ties so deep,*
*A lineage through which pure bloodlines sweep.*

*Her father Khuwaylid's name held in esteem,*
*And from her mother's side, a noble stream.*
*His mother, Amna[70], shared these honored roots,*
*For Barrah[71], too, in grandeur bore its fruits.*

*She sent him forth to lands on distant trails,*
*She saw his virtues, pure as angel's sails.*
*A trading star, his brilliance shone so bright,*
*She sought his hand to make her heart's delight.*

*His worth, his honesty, so pure and clear,*
*She knew that he was meant for her near.*
*In pride and grace, she sent the bold request,*
*To claim the one whose virtues were the best.*

---

[70] Amna: The mother of Prophet Muhammad (PBUH). She passed away when he was young, leaving him an orphan.
[71] Barrah: The mother of Umm Ayman, a close companion of Khadijah and servant of Prophet Muhammad (PBUH), who continued to serve the Prophet after Khadijah's death.

*Her house, like lions, stood in strength and fame,*
*And yet her heart was drawn to just his name.*
*No wealth or pride could match the man he'd be,*
*For in his soul, true greatness she did see.*

*Thus, Khadija, rich in trade and light,*
*Became the one who matched his heart so bright.*
*Together they would forge a path so clear,*
*A union blessed, a love sincere and dear.*

## *A Model for All Eternity*

*In the humble home, a guiding light,
The Prophet worked from dawn till night.
Not one to command, nor to demand,
He lent his heart and offered his hand.*

*He mended his clothes, stitched with care,
Swept the floor, and dusted the air.
Milk he drew, his chores he'd share,
A husband's love, beyond compare.*

*With Aisha, his laughter would bloom,
A joy that filled the modest room.
Gentle words, so soft, so sweet,
In her presence, his love complete.*

*One day they raced, the earth their field,
Aisha's speed the first to yield.
Years passed by, they raced once more,
This time he won; his playful score.*

*He'd help prepare the meal with grace,
No task too small, no role debased.
For he taught us all, by word and deed,
That love is sharing, the truest creed.*

*The best of men, as he proclaimed,
Are those to their wives, in kindness famed.
And he, the best of them by far,
A guiding light, our shining star.*

*Muhammad, the perfect husband, he,
A model for all eternity.*

## Compassion, Honesty and Forgiveness

*Compassion flowed from heart to hand,*
*For all creation, every land.*
*He showed the world a mercy pure,*
*For animals, the weak, the poor.*
*The trees, the earth, the skies above,*
*All felt the warmth of his great love.*

*Honesty, a shining light,*
*"Al-Amin," in truth and right.*
*In every dealing, fair and clear,*
*No soul could doubt his words sincere.*
*Integrity, his guiding way,*
*In every night, in every day.*

*Forgiveness, boundless, filled his soul,*
*He made the broken-hearted whole.*
*Enemies became his friends,*
*Through his mercy, hatred ends.*
*He taught the power to forgive,*
*Is how a soul in peace should live.*

*Humility, despite his fame,*
*He lived as one, with no great claim.*
*In simple homes, with tasks he'd share,*
*A leader's heart, so just and fair.*
*He walked among, not high above,*
*And taught the world of selfless love.*

## *Justice, Patience and Generosity*

*Justice ruled his every word,*
*And fairness in his heart was heard.*
*The high, the low, were equal here,*
*No man of status did he fear.*
*For truth and justice, he would stand,*
*A guiding light in every land.*

*Patience through the trials of life,*
*He stood with strength amidst the strife.*
*Through hardship, pain, and long delay,*
*He kept his faith and paved the way.*
*His patience taught the world to see,*
*In every storm, there's victory.*

*Generosity without end,*
*He gave to all, from foe to friend.*
*His hand would never turn away,*
*The beggar's plea, the poor man's day.*
*With open heart and humble mind,*
*He shared his wealth with all mankind.*

*Politeness marked his every tone,*
*Respect for all, his actions shown.*
*In every word, in every deed,*
*He cared for every soul in need.*

## *The Profound Humility*

*So humble was he, though the earth did know,*
*The best of all that here below could grow.*

*He ascends to the heavens, the seventh divine,*
*Then returns to the earth, in humble design.*
*With sandals trimmed, he tends to his sheep,*
*And dines with the poor, their sorrows he keeps.*

*Such are the nobles, in wisdom they rise,*
*Yet even in greatness, they wear no disguise.*
*With companions around him, a feast to prepare,*
*"I'll slaughter the sheep!" cries the first with a flare.*
*"I will cook it!" says another, with pride in his heart,*
*"I'll gather the wood," our Prophet replies,*
*In the heart of true adults, selflessness lies.*

*With riches in hand, he calls to the throng,*
*Yet forgets his own self, where shadows belong.*
*In armor he faces a fate bitter and steep,*
*Yet clings to the truth, where silence runs deep.*

*O Abu Hurairah[72], witness wisdom unfold,*
*In prayer, he kneels, both humble and bold.*
*Upon his dear grandson, Al-Hassan he leans,*
*Their bond shining bright in their sacred routines.*

*A child's gentle cry cuts through the still air,*
*He shortens his prayer, showing deep, tender care.*

---

[72] Abu Hurairah: a prominent companion of Prophet Muhammad (PBUH) known for his vast knowledge and numerous hadiths (sayings of the Prophet).

*For mercy is found where compassion flows free,*
*In the heart of our prophet, his kindness we see.*

## *A Man of Wisdom, Strength, and Peace*

**Zaid bin Thabit [73] sat close by,**
*Recording words from the Prophet's eye.*
*In moments of divine decree,*
*He learned how life and faith agree.*
*Worldly matters, work, and trade,*
*With honesty and mercy were laid,*
*For Prophet Muhammad showed the way,*
*To blend the earth with skies each day.*

**In every action, big or small,**
*The Prophet linked it to the call,*
*That even food and daily strife,*
*Were connected to a higher life.*
*He balanced both the worldly field,*
*And spiritual truths that wouldn't yield.*

**Then Amr [74] once asked, "Who is best?"**
*The Prophet, with truth in his chest,*
*Named Abu Bakr, Umar too,*
*Uthman's name then swiftly flew.*
*Though kind at heart, his words were clear,*
*For truth was always held sincere.*

---

[73] Zaid bin Thabit: A devoted companion of Prophet Muhammad (PBUH), known for his expertise in writing and preserving the Quran, playing a key role in its compilation.

[74] Amr: A companion of Prophet Muhammad (PBUH), known for his contributions to early Islamic conquests and his role in spreading Islam.

**But wisdom ruled his honest way,**
He'd speak when asked, but never betray
Nor cause needless hurt, nor painful sting;
His truthfulness made wisdom sing.
He knew when silence was the key,
And when to set the truth words free.

**Anas bin Malik [75] served him well,**
Ten years beside him, he could tell
The patience, gentleness, and care,
The Prophet's heart was always fair.
No anger, no complaint arose,
For in his soul, pure mercy flows.

*A man of wisdom, strength, and peace,*
*Whose love and truth shall never cease.*

---

[75] Anas bin Malik: A close companion of Prophet Muhammad (PBUH), known for his service to the Prophet and for narrating over 2,000 hadiths, preserving much of the Prophet's teachings.

## *Muhammad's Light Shone Everywhere*

Ali spoke of his patience, vast and true,
With every soul, the Prophet knew,
He'd sit and listen, give them time,
Never leaving, no matter the climb.
No rush, no haste, no sign of stress,
Until they left with their heart at rest.

Generosity shone in all his ways,
Even in the busiest of days.
No matter how tired or pressed for time,
He'd lend his ear, so pure, sublime.
A compassion so deep, so rare to find,
A heart so giving, gentle, and kind.

If you asked of him, you'd not depart,
Without some solace, soothing the heart.
If he had it, he'd give without delay,
And if not, kind words would light your way.
Never a refusal, never a 'no,'
In his mercy, endless streams would flow.

To those in need, his kindness poured,
No harsh dismissal, but love restored.
Even those deemed unworthy by men,
He'd treat with respect, again and again.
For he knew, in asking, there's often pain,
And with gentleness, dignities regained.

Thus, in patience, grace, and endless care,
Muhammad's light shone everywhere.

## *Servitude Over Throne*

*A kingly crown, a kingdom in his hand,*
*God gave him choice, but see how pure he stands.*
*He could have ruled with wealth and golden might,*
*Yet chose to serve, to guide us in the light.*

*The mountains of the earth, with treasures vast,*
*Were placed before him, riches unsurpassed.*
*Gold from the veins of Arabia's soil,*
*But he refused, untouched by worldly spoil.*

*He knew the wealth would come, but not for him,*
*A trial for his people, bright yet grim.*
*"The doors will open, treasures will unfold,*
*The wealth of Caesar, stores of ancient gold."*

*But in his heart, no greed did ever grow,*
*He warned of dangers wealth can bring below.*
*"My brothers," he said, "I fear not for your souls,*
*Except from what the world will soon unroll.*

*The flower of the earth, so sweet, so bright,*
*It tempts the heart, and blinds it to the light.*
*Like trees that flourish, green beneath the sun,*
*But wither once the heat has fully won.*

*For wealth can drain the soul of what is pure,*
*Its grip is fleeting, never can endure.*
*But blessed are they who give without a fear,*
*Who feed the poor and hold the needy dear."*

*Though gold bowed to him, in faith he stood so tall,*

*The richest of the rich, yet free from all.*
*faith was his wealth, his treasure rare,*
*A prophet-servant, humble in his care.*

*His warning echoes still, through time and land,*
*That worldly riches slip like desert sand.*
*Yet he, the richest, in his heart did find,*
*A wealth of spirit, strong, unchained, refined.*

## *His Leadership*

*A leader kind, a gentle face,*
*With perfect manners, filled with grace.*

*His leadership, with wisdom bright,*
*He guided others through the night.*
*He led with counsel, care, and thought,*
*In every action, wisdom sought.*
*He stood with courage, firm and true,*
*When dangers came, he always knew.*

*Sincerity was in his heart,*
*In every role, he played his part.*
*With empathy for all who came,*
*He felt their joy, he felt their pain.*
*Modesty adorned his way,*
*In every act, from night to day.*

*Gratitude in every breath,*
*He thanked his Lord until his death.*
*He taught the world to see and trust,*
*That in God's plan, we must adjust.*
*Trustworthiness, in every pact,*
*No one could doubt his honest act.*

*Fairness in trade, he would ensure,*
*That dealings were just, and always pure.*
*For women's rights, he did defend,*
*And stood as both their guide and friend.*
*With love for children, kind and warm,*
*He sheltered them through every storm.*

*The earth he honored, cared for well,*
*In stewardship, his words would tell.*
*He sought for knowledge, wisdom bright,*
*Encouraging minds to seek the light.*
*These virtues live, in hearts today,*
*A timeless guide, a righteous way.*

## *Muhammad Shines as The Master of Balance*

*Three men approached with zeal but hearts confused,*
*Each one extreme in ways they had pursued.*
*They sought to fast, to pray beyond the norm,*
*To live without the joys that life had borne.*

*Yet in his wisdom, Muhammad calmly spoke,*
*"A balanced path, the middle way, invoke.*
*For faith is not in hardship's heavy chain,*
*But in a heart that knows both joy and pain."*

*He taught that moderation brings the light,*
*That in the middle path, our faith shines bright.*
*Like gentle winds that cool the desert's heat,*
*His words of truth made every soul complete.*

*Muhammad, like the sun in skies so wide,*
*The light by which all life on earth abides.*
*No stone that's thrown by hands of those who scorn,*
*Can ever dim the light from which we're drawn.*

*For fools may speak, yet still the sun will rise,*
*And cast its beams across the endless skies.*
*Like children tossing stones that never land,*
*Their words fall short, for none can dim his stand.*

*So let them try, but know his light remains,*
*Beyond the reach of envy's futile chains.*
*For even angels, pure as they may be,*
*Had those who scorned their grace and dignity.*

*The Ashrafiya Hymn*            *Dr. Ashi Ezz*

*Muhammad shines, a light ever true,*
*To guide our hearts in all we say and do.*
*No stone nor word can steal the light away,*
*He rises still, to bring the dawn of day.*

## *Perfection in Every Touch:*
## *The Finest Form*

*Behold Muhammad, blessed, pure, and true,*
*The finest form that ever heaven knew.*
*In stature, none could stand as fair and tall,*
*In character, he shines beyond them all.*

*God placed him in the highest state of grace,*
*The best of form, the most beloved face.*
*He shaped his soul with virtues rare and bright,*
*And crowned him as creation's perfect light.*

*In honored time, from lineage divine,*
*He stood as man's most noble, sacred sign.*
*The age he lived, the finest ever told,*
*His nation, like him, pure as burnished gold.*

*The best companions walked beside his way,*
*The truest hearts that heard what he would say.*
*And of his wives, the finest God did choose,*
*The ones whose love the Prophet could not lose.*

*To him, God sent the greatest book of all,*
*The Quran, on which all mankind may call.*
*Its laws the purest, guiding every deed,*
*A path for all who search and all who need.*

*His every step, the closest to God's will,*
*In every act, his purpose shining still.*
*For God himself did shape him and refine,*
*And made his actions wholly pure, divine.*

*Muhammad, disciplined and trained with care,*
*The highest model, far beyond compare.*
*For he, in all his being, stands apart;*
*Among the most beloved to God's heart.*

## *Muhammad: The Eternal Flame*

*Muhammad, noblest of both Arab and non-Arab lands,*
*A light who walked the earth with steady hands.*
*In every step, in every deed,*
*He spread goodness, fulfilling the deepest need.*

*With kindness unmatched, and generosity wide,*
*He wore the crown of God's messengers with pride.*
*Truth in his words, firm in his vow,*
*His essence, eternal light even now.*

*From the first breath of creation, he was pure light,*
*Shattering the darkness, making the path bright.*
*A ruler just, with honor keen,*
*A wellspring of blessings, serene and clean.*

*From Mudar's lineage, the finest grace,*
*Among God's prophets, he took his place.*
*His message true, a warning clear,*
*A figure so distinct, held forever dear.*

*His name, it breathes life into every soul,*
*Binding us to gratitude, making us whole.*
*The world itself adorned by his grace,*
*Erasing every shadow, filling every space.*

*His virtues, clean of every stain,*
*Fashioned by the Merciful, without disdain.*

*The chosen one, a light so true,*
*That pierced the veil of the darkest blue.*

*He smiled at guests, open and kind,*
*With a heart that sheltered all of mankind.*
*In his mission, no falter, no retreat,*
*Bringing wisdom to the world's feet.*

*On the final Day, when all must plead,*
*He will stand for his people in their greatest need.*
*The last of the prophets, the seal divine,*
*Muhammad; our beacon, forever to shine.*

*Blessed by God in form and name,*
*A legacy etched in an eternal flame.*

*Allah's love for him shines so bright,*
*A bond eternal, a guiding light.*
*In every prayer, his name is known,*
*With Allah's own, it stands alone.*

*The Shahada [76]echoes, a truth so clear,*
*"None but Allah," and "Muhammad, dear."*
*In every call, the Adhan's sweet chime,*
*Honors the Prophet more than once each time.*

*Five daily prayers, nine times we say,*
*His name resounds in our hearts' array.*
*A bond unbroken, divine and pure,*
*A love eternal, forever secure.*

---

[76] Shahada: The Islamic declaration of faith, stating "There is no god but Allah, and Muhammad is the messenger of Allah." It is the fundamental testimony of belief in Islam.

### *The Five Reasons We Love Him So*

1. Perfection in Creation, pure and bright,
He was formed in beauty, radiant light,
Chosen from the finest line,
In the best of lands and sacred time.
Above all prophets, angels, creation's gleam,
He stood honored in God's grand dream.

2. His Character, noble, unmatched and high,
In every word, in every sigh,
A model of morals, truth, and grace,
He set the standard, time cannot erase.
A heart so gentle, pure, and kind,
With every virtue perfectly aligned.

3. His Benevolence, like rain from above,
A mercy to all, a beacon of love.
From darkness to light, his message brought,
Guiding us to the truth we sought.
The best of nations he made from dust,
By teaching compassion, faith, and trust.

4. Our Hope, in him, on Judgment Day,
For his intercession, we humbly pray.
In paradise, by his side we'll stand,
With endless bliss in a promised land.
His presence brings hope, pure and true,
A future bright for me, for you.

5. The Relationship, deeper than blood's embrace,
More worthy of love than any face.

*The Ashrafiya Hymn*                 *Dr. Ashi Ezz*

*He is to us more than a father near,*
*A bond that grows without fear.*
*His wives, our mothers, honored and dear,*
*In his love, we find peace and cheer.*

*So, five reasons our hearts incline,*
*To love him, follow, and align.*
*In every step, in every prayer,*
*Muhammad's love, beyond compare.*

# Section 3: Glimpse of His Daily life

## *A Glimpse of What He Wore and Eat*

*He loved the simple joys that life revealed,*
*A humble soul, content with each meal.*
*If he liked the food, he'd eat with grace,*
*If not, no harsh words would take its place.*

*Milk was his choice, a drink of pure delight,*
*A taste of calm, refreshing through the night.*

*Then meat he favored, rich in tender grace,*
*The arm and forearm held the highest place.*
*He savored squash, both yellow, red, and fair,*
*From earth's sweet fruits, he took his tender care.*

*His clothes were pure, in Arab style he'd stand,*
*With robes and buttons from a sacred hand.*
*Like Abraham, in garments rich and true,*
*A timeless grace within his garments grew.*

*When gifts of clothes were brought from near and far,*
*He wore them too, each one a precious star.*
*Pants graced his form, a gift he wore with pride,*
*In every stitch, his humble heart did bide.*

*In sandals crafted from the finest hide,*
*Black leather brought from Egypt's flowing tide.*
*With simple shoes, he walked the desert wide,*
*A man of grace, with modesty as guide.*

*Through all he wore and all he chose to eat,*
*His humble soul made every act complete.*

*A teacher true, in every choice and deed,*
*In life's small things, he sowed the finest seed.*

## *The Prophet's Companions*

*His Companions knew his bond with God above,*
*A tie of reverence, praise, and deepest love.*
*In modest awe before his Lord he stood,*
*His heart in worship pure, his will to good.*

*With every breath, he glorified His Lord name,*
*His lips in constant praise, a humble flame.*
*To God he turned with love beyond compare,*
*In every act, devotion rich and rare.*

*His Companions watched, and in their hearts it grew,*
*A love so deep, their loyalty so true.*
*As Urwa said, like birds upon their heads,*
*They sat in silence, still as one who treads.*

*No lip would move, no eye would dare to blink,*
*They stood as though on holy ground to think.*
*In awe of him, whose every word they sought,*
*Their hearts in reverence, with love so taught.*

*Like camels calm with birds upon their crown,*
*They stayed unmoved when his words trickled down.*
*No shifting gaze, no restless step or sound,*
*Just love for him in every soul was found.*

*For in his speech, they heard the truth so clear,*
*A guide from God they cherished and held dear.*
*Their love for him was more than words can say,*
*A bond of light that time could not betray.*

## *Mecca; Medina and Al-Aqsa in His Heart*

*God Almighty honored him with grace,
In three lands blessed by His embrace.*

*Mecca, cradle of his noble birth,
Where faith ignited on sacred earth.
Thirteen years of steadfast call,
A source of truth, a city beloved by all.
Revelation's light first kissed the air,
A timeless truth beyond compare.*

*To Al-Aqsa's sanctity, he rose one night,
Through veils of splendor, bathed in light.
A meeting with prophets, a prayer sublime,
A moment eternal, transcending time.*

*Then Medina, his home, a chosen place,
A city of faith, of love, and grace.
Ten wondrous years of patience and light,
Where hearts united, wrong turned right.
Its soil embraced him, its streets he blessed,
In life and death, his place of rest.*

*Twenty-three years, the Prophethood span,
The best of times for all of man.
A period of mercy, unmatched, profound,
When heaven's wisdom walked the ground.*

*Three lands exalted, bound by decree,
In their embrace, God's light we see.*

*The Ashrafiya Hymn* — *Dr. Ashi Ezz*

## *Friday*

*This time, a season of heavenly delight,*
*When God bestowed His mercy, pure and bright.*
*And Friday, blessed above all days of lore,*
*The day creation's tale began its core.*

*On Friday Adam was formed from divine clay,*
*Descended, repented, and passed away.*
*The day of reckoning, too, will rise,*
*Beneath the watching, waiting skies.*

*No beast nor bird but stirs at morning's crest,*
*Aware that Friday is divinely blessed.*
*Save man and jinn, who wander unaware,*
*Of the Hour approaching in the air.*

*So, send your prayers upon Muhammad's name,*
*For each prayer brings a blessing to your flame.*
*A day of guidance, when past nations strayed,*
*But God led this nation, and His truth displayed.*

*Oh God, bless Muhammad, grand and pure,*
*Equal to the prayers from your creations and more.*
*From the first uttered word to the final call,*
*Though I believe it shall never fade at all.*

## *Muhammad's Personal Hygiene*

*In days of old, where shadows fell,*
*Prophet Muhammad's stories swell.*
*His hair was groomed with tender care,*
*A sign of love, so pure and rare.*

*Aisha, in her reverence, would comb,*
*Even in times of discomfort's home.*
*Her actions challenged ancient lore,*
*Restoring women's worth once more.*
*His compassion, strong and profound.*

*Oil he used with fragrant grace,*
*His hair and beard, a well-kept place.*
*A qun'ah shielded his attire,*
*From stains, his neatness did inspire.*
*People spoke of his sweet scent,*
*Like a perfumed merchant, heaven-sent.*

*In every act, from left to right,*
*Starting with the right, a gentle light.*
*His grooming, modest, balanced, wise,*
*With no excess to disguise.*
*His care was neither vain nor loud,*
*But a reflection of a humble proud.*

*Gray hair adorned with few in sight,*
*not more 20 strands, a symbol bright.*
*He chose not dyes to hide the hue,*
*Leaving nature's grace in view.*

*Abu Bakr's hues of henna bright,*
*Were a contrast to his natural light.*

*Thus, in his care, a lesson lies,*
*Of modesty that never dies.*
*With each detail, from hair to grace,*
*Muhammad's love touched every space.*

## *From Radiant Face to Grace Walk*

*In the desert's sunlit blaze,*
*Muhammad's stride was set ablaze.*
*His walk, a mix of light and grace,*
*With a radiant, sunlit face.*

*A swiftness marked his every stride,*
*With focus deep, and purpose wide.*
*His gait was steady, strong, profound,*
*Each step a journey, heaven-bound.*

*Leaders of the modern day,*
*With commanding steps that sway,*
*Reflect a presence strong and clear,*
*Yet none compare to the Prophet's sphere.*

*His attire, a testament to care,*
*A head covering, both fine and rare.*
*To keep his hair and garb pristine,*
*Fragrant and clean, a noble sheen.*

*In every step, in every line,*
*A leader's grace, both rare and fine.*
*From radiant face to grace walk,*
*In every detail, his virtues talk.*

## The Prophet's Gathformations

*In gatherings calm, where peace held sway,*
*Ali spoke of truths in plain array.*
*The Prophet's voice, serene, refined,*
*Brought comfort deep to heart and mind.*

*With patient tone, his wisdom spread,*
*Each word a balm where justice led.*
*No voice was raised, no anger near,*
*But respect graced the atmosphere.*

*With hearts inclined, the crowd would heed,*
*His words, a light for every need.*
*For Allah spoke, and made it clear,*
*Reverence for him must persevere.*

*To raise a voice was grave indeed,*
*It cast aside one's righteous deed.*
*Yet in his gatherings, light was shown,*
*With dignity for all, well-known.*

*The sinner, stranger, the pure too,*
*Were met with kindness firm and true.*
*Should manners stray or errors fall,*
*His gentle hand would mend them all.*

*No wealth or rank could set apart,*
*A soul unclean from pious heart.*
*For he illustrated, all worth was weighed,*
*By faith, not earthly wealth displayed.*

*He fed the poor, gave care to all,*
*And answered every earnest call.*

The Ashrafiya Hymn                                    Dr. Ashi Ezz

*A life of service, pure and bright,*
*His gatherings were heaven's light.*

*Through humble ways, he'd always teach,*
*That love and justice all could reach.*
*In every soul, his flame would glow,*
*A mercy for the world to know.*

# Section 4: Some of His Miracles

## *From Stones to Trees, From Dust to Grain*

In the palm of his hand, pebbles lay,
Yet they glorified God in their own way.
Muhammad passed them, one by one,
To Abu Bakr, Omar, and Uthman.

In each hand, they praised the Lord,
A sign of leadership, divinely restored.

And when food was set before their eyes,
It too, sang praise, a wondrous surprise.
As they ate, the tasbih rang clear,
God's glory was present, ever near.

In Mecca's streets, stones would greet,
Muhammad's steps, so calm and sweet.
"Peace be upon you, O Messenger of God,"
The rocks would whisper where he trod.

Mountains stood tall, trees stood firm,
Yet even they, to the Prophet, turned.
With "Salaam" they bowed, they knew his name,
Honoring the one with divine flame.

On Badr's plain, the battle fierce,
A handful of dust, through air did pierce.
Muhammad threw, and by God's might,
The Muslims triumphed in the fight.

*At Hunayn's [77]clash, the scene was grim,*
*Yet pebbles flew from the hand of him.*
*A command was given, swift and true,*
*Victory followed with skies so blue.*

*A palm trunk wept, with love so deep,*
*When from its side, the Prophet did leap.*
*It missed his touch, his gentle lean,*
*Until he comforted its unseen.*
*A trunk that cried, with yearning bark,*
*For the Prophet's heart left its mark.*

*From stones to trees, from dust to grain,*
*The miracles of Muhammad remain.*
*In every act, God's hand we see,*
*A testament to His Prophet's decree.*

---

[77] Hunayn's: Refers to the Battle of Hunayn, fought between the early Muslims and the tribes of Hawazin and Thaqif. It was a significant victory for the Muslims, demonstrating both challenges and triumphs in the early Islamic period.

*The Ashrafiya Hymn*     *Dr. Ashi Ezz*

## *Miracles with Food and Drinks*

*When poverty struck, hunger pressed,*
*Companions starved, their faith undressed.*
*Abu Hurairah, in hunger's grip,*
*Saw a miracle, from the Prophet's lip.*

*A bowl of milk, too small to share,*
*Yet through the Prophet's loving care,*
*It passed through hands, from one to all,*
*And each drank deeply, none left small.*

*Obedience showed in Hurairah's plight,*
*Though hunger gnawed, he saw the light.*
*He called the people, filled with trust,*
*In God's provision, fair and just.*

*Generous Prophet, always near,*
*He gave to those who had no cheer.*
*The people of Suffah* [78]*knew his heart,*
*For with them, he'd never part.*

*When Abu Talha's* [79]*wife prepared,*
*A meal so small, the Prophet dared*

---

[78] Suffah: A platform in the mosque of Medina where a group of companions, known as the Ahl al-Suffah, lived. They were dedicated to learning from the Prophet Muhammad (PBUH) and were known for their piety and devotion.

[79] Abu Talha's: A companion of Prophet Muhammad (PBUH), known for his deep faith and generosity. He is especially remembered for his contributions during the Battle of Uhud, where he defended the Prophet with great bravery.

*To call the many to their feast,*
*And by his blessing, food increased.*

*And Jabir's[80] palm trees bore their fruit,*
*To pay his father's debt in suit.*
*The Prophet's hand upon the tree,*
*Ensured their bounty, set him free.*

*When water lacked, no stream in sight,*
*The Prophet raised his hand of light.*
*From between his fingers, clear as day,*
*Water flowed, to wash, to pray.*
*A miracle, a blessing true,*
*For all to drink, for all who knew.*

*With barley small, enough for few,*
*He fed the hungry; a mighty crew.*
*Abu Talha saw seventy fed,*
*While from little, their bellies spread.*
*And on the day of the trench, with care,*
*One thousand men shared barley and prayer.*
*From just one goat, the Prophet's hand,*
*Nourished them, a feast so grand.*

*Abu Ayyub[81], with food for two,*
*Saw one hundred eighty men come through.*

---

[80] Jabir's: Refers to Jabir bin Abdullah, a companion of Prophet Muhammad (PBUH), known for his contributions to the narration of hadiths and his involvement in significant events like the Battle of Uhud. He is particularly remembered for his role in the transmission of knowledge and Islamic teachings.

[81] Abu Ayyub: A companion of Prophet Muhammad (PBUH), known for his hospitality and loyalty. He hosted the Prophet in his home when he first arrived in Medina and later participated in key battles such as the Battle of Yarmouk.

*With the Prophet's grace, the meal expanded,*
*And every man left full and handed.*

*Water flowed from between his hands,*
*A miracle for all the lands.*
*Three hundred souls ablution found,*
*Where once no drops were to be found.*
*Milk and food increased in share,*
*The Prophet's blessing, always fair.*

*In every word, in every deed,*
*Muhammad met each faithful need.*
*His prophecies and miracles stand,*
*A mercy sent by God's own hand.*

## *Miracles of Healing and the Power of His Prayers*

*In battle fierce, an eye did fall,*
*Qatadah's [82]sight was gone with all.*
*But with one touch, the Prophet healed,*
*Restoring vision, strong and sealed.*
*And wounds from arrows, sharp and red,*
*He healed with spit, the bloodlines fled.*

*For Anas, a prayer was made,*
*His wealth and kin, in full cascade.*
*Abd al-Rahman[83], with riches vast,*
*The Prophet's words, a future cast.*
*Muawiyah [84]rose with power great,*
*A caliph's fate, the Prophet's state.*
*Saad[85], with prayers that never failed,*
*His supplications always hailed.*

---

[82] Qatadah's: Refers to Qatadah bin al-Nu'man, a companion of Prophet Muhammad (PBUH), known for his wisdom and participation in early Islamic battles. He is remembered for his contributions to the spread of Islamic knowledge and his role in various key events in Islamic history.

[83] Abd al-Rahman bin Awf, one of the wealthiest and most generous companions of Prophet Muhammad (PBUH). He played a key role in early Islamic expansion and was known for his philanthropy and business acumen.

[84] Muawiyah: A prominent companion of Prophet Muhammad (PBUH) and the founder of the Umayyad dynasty. Known for his leadership, Muawiyah played a significant role in early Islamic history, particularly in the establishment of the caliphate and his involvement in the Battle of Siffin.

[85] Saad: Refers to Saad bin Abi Waqqas, a companion of Prophet Muhammad (PBUH) and a prominent military leader.

*And as for prophecies, he saw,*
*Events to come, with perfect law.*
*The Day of Judgment, far yet near,*
*His words remembered, crystal clear.*

*Through miracles, his path was shown,*
*A mercy from the Unseen Throne.*
*In every act, in every sign,*
*The Prophet lived by God's design.*

## Miracles of Rain and Provision

*In drought's dry grip, the people came,*
*Their lands were parched, their crops aflame.*
*A man, with hope, raised his plea,*
*"O Prophet, pray for rain for thee."*
*The Prophet raised his hands on high,*
*And soon the clouds filled the sky.*
*Six days of rain, abundant grace,*
*The land revived, a watered place.*

*Yet the man returned, the fields now drowned,*
*"Too much, O Prophet, the waters surround."*
*The Prophet prayed once more for peace,*
*For rain to fall, but troubles cease.*
*Around them then the rain did pour,*
*But not a drop where they stood no more.*

*In Tabuk'[86]s heat, the army faint,*
*With thirst so dire, their steps grew faint.*
*Abu Bakr called, the Prophet heard,*
*And with his prayer, the skies were stirred.*
*Only where the soldiers stood,*
*Rain descended, pure and good.*

*The Quraysh once faced a drought so grave,*
*Their lands could not, the famine stave.*

---

[86] Tabuk: Refers to the Battle of Tabuk, a significant military expedition led by Prophet Muhammad (PBUH) against the Byzantine forces in 630 CE. It was one of the last major campaigns during the Prophet's lifetime, marking the strength of the growing Islamic state.

*Abu Sufyan, in desperate strife,*
*Sought the Prophet to restore life.*
*A prayer was said, the drought was gone,*
*The mercy of God, in rains drawn on.*

*Through every storm and drying ground,*
*His prayers brought rain, his mercy found.*
*A sign of God's love, pure and bright,*
*Through Muhammad, the guiding light.*

## His Prophecies

*In the shadows of prophecy, wisdom unfolds,*
*The Prophet foretold trials, as the future he told.*
*Marvelous truths in his words, a light to behold,*
*Some have come to pass, and some yet to unfold.*

*He spoke of Mecca's doors, flung open wide,*
*Foretelling conquest with God as guide.*
*Yemen, Levant, and Iraq in view,*
*Each prophecy spoken, in time, proved true.*

*The Holy City gained through his reign,*
*Or after his passing, all blessings attained.*
*At Khaybar's gate stood bold Ali's might,*
*The promise fulfilled with dawn's first light.*

*The treasures of Caesar and Khosrau too,*
*Foretold by Muhammad, came into view.*
*In Omar's time, the riches poured,*
*As kings' spoils were brought and stored.*

*He spoke of his foes and their destined end,*
*Of Badr's field where each would descend.*
*He foretold Umar's martyrdom, Ali's last stand,*
*And Uthman's unjust death by discord's hand.*

*He warned of the Camel's battle[87], of kin turned foe,*

---

[87] Camel's Battle: Refers to the Battle of the Camel, fought in 656 CE between forces loyal to Caliph Ali and those led by Talha, and Zubair, seeking justice for the assassination of the third caliph, Uthman. It was a pivotal conflict in early Islamic history, highlighting internal divisions within the Muslim community.

*Of nations feasting upon us, our strength laid low.*
*Wealth unchecked, values turned to dust,*
*Arabs competing, towers rise as a must.*

*The slave gives birth to her master's pride,*
*While knowledge spreads, and gluttony grows wide.*
*Women clothed yet bare, shame across the land,*
*Trade flourishes aimlessly, wealth in ladies' hands.*

*Violence rampant, blood taints the earth,*
*Music ascends, vices laugh in mirth.*
*Syria besieged, its faithful in despair,*
*All he foretold emerges everywhere.*

*These, for sure, we all can see;*
*Blind who not to trust what's yet to be.*

*A war with Rome, as allies then foes,*
*Euphrates' gold revealed, igniting human woes.*
*The Mahdi [88]will reign, restoring the just,*
*The Caliphate returns, fulfilling the trust.*

*Dajjal's [89]deceit, then Isa descends,*
*Gog and Magog rage until their end.*
*Smoke will veil the sky; the earth will quake,*
*Mecca and Medina, their sanctity will break.*

---

[88] Mahdi: In Islamic eschatology, the Mahdi is a messianic figure who is expected to appear before the Day of Judgment to restore justice, peace, and righteousness. His arrival is believed to be a sign of the end times, guiding Muslims in a period of spiritual renewal.

[89] Dajjal's: Refers to the Dajjal, a deceptive, evil figure in Islamic eschatology, often described as the false messiah. He will appear during the end times, leading many astray, before being defeated by the Mahdi and Jesus (Isa) in a final battle between good and evil.

*The Beast will speak, the sun will rise in the west,*
*A gentle breeze will take the faithful to rest.*
*The Qur'an will rise; the Kaaba turns to dust,*
*A fire will guide the lost, as destiny must.*

*And when the hour strikes, only the wicked remain,*
*On them will fall eternal loss and pain.*
*Prophecies unfold from wisdom's call,*
*Who dares deny the truth of it all?*

*The beloved one, the ultimate true,*
*Through his warnings, salvation renews.*

## *A Testament to His Divine Place*

*The Qur'an, a light, unmatched and grand,*
*With wisdom deep for every land.*
*Its words, like stars, forever bright,*
*Revealing secrets in the night.*
*Unchanged through time, its truth remains,*
*A guide for hearts, through joy and pains.*
*Science, law, and eloquence clear,*
*Its miracles forever near.*

*The Isra, Mi'raj, a journey high,*
*Through heavens vast, beyond the sky.*
*From Mecca's heart to Jerusalem's dome,*
*He ascended to where souls roam.*
*Through every level, prophets greet,*
*Till with God, he took his seat.*
*A journey that no man could claim,*
*Yet by God's will, Muhammad's fame.*

*The moon did split, the skies did part,*
*A sign to soften every heart.*
*The Meccans saw the moon divide,*
*Witnessed by those both far and wide.*
*A miracle in the night's embrace,*
*A sign of God's enduring grace.*

*Water flowed from between his hands,*
*A miracle across the sands.*
*His companions drank and washed with glee,*
*A spring of mercy, pure and free.*

*From fingers blessed, life's gift did flow,*
*A sign of grace, for all to know.*

*The tree trunk wept, its love so pure,*
*For the Prophet, its bond was sure.*
*He leaned on it in every speech,*
*But cried when it was out of reach.*
*Such tenderness, a love so strong,*
*Even nature knew he belonged.*

*With a prayer, the rain did fall,*
*A mercy sent, answering the call.*
*For six long days, the land was wet,*
*And on the seventh, sunshine set.*
*His prayers were heard in every need,*
*A miracle for hearts to heed.*

*He prayed, and healing softly came,*
*To ease the hurt, to lift the lame.*
*The blind saw light, the broken stood,*
*Through him, God's mercy flowed like flood.*
*Each whispered prayer, a balm, a guide,*
*Revealed compassion deep and wide.*

*The animals, they knew his grace,*
*The camel bowed, a humble face.*
*It knelt before the Prophet's feet,*
*And spoke of sorrows none could meet.*
*For mistreatment it did bemoan,*
*Yet with Muhammad, it found a home.*

*A wolf proclaimed what few could see,*
*That Muhammad's truth was prophecy.*
*With witness rare from beastly kind,*
*It testified, with heart and mind.*

*For even creatures knew his worth,*
*A mercy sent upon this earth.*

*Miracles with food and drink,*
*A sign from God that makes us think.*
*From little barley, masses fed,*
*With just a prayer, the hungry sped.*
*And water from his fingers streamed,*
*A blessing rare, as heaven gleamed.*

*His words foretold of future days,*
*Of lands to come and changing ways.*
*Each prophecy, a truth divine,*
*That time and fate would both align.*
*And history tells of what he said,*
*As one by one, his words were read.*

*These miracles, these signs of light,*
*They fill our hearts with awe and might.*
*Through skies, through land, through nature's grace,*
*A testament to his divine place.*

*For in Muhammad's life, we find,*
*God's endless mercy to mankind.*

# Section 5: The Light of His Being

### *His Skin: The Glow of Grace*

*A complexion kissed by sun and breeze,*
*Fair, yet touched with warmth to please.*
*Not pale, nor harsh, but softly bright,*
*A radiance pure, a glowing light.*

*A hint of rose in every hue,*
*A blush of life in all he'd do.*
*Like dawn's first glow upon the land,*
*A warmth so gentle, yet so grand.*

*His skin, though tested by desert's heat,*
*Retained a freshness, smell so sweet.*
*For even sun, with all its might,*
*Could not wither the Prophet's light.*

*"Bayad Mushrab"[90], the poets say,*
*A glow that never fades away.*
*He walked with grace, his skin aglow,*
*Reflecting mercy, calm and slow.*

*In every step, a breeze of peace,*
*A beauty that would never cease.*
*For in his face, a truth divine,*
*A light that shone, a holy sign.*

---

[90] Bayad Mushrab: white mix with a perfect red

### *His Hair: A Silver Thread*

*His hair, like waves of gentle night,*
*Softly flowing, a velvet sight.*
*Cascading down to ear or shoulder,*
*In every strand, the world grew bolder.*

*Black as ink that shades the skies,*
*With a gleam that caught a thousand eyes.*
*Sometimes parted, neatly kept,*
*In its embrace, even winds slept.*

*Dark and flowing, calm, refined,*
*A perfect blend of heart and mind.*
*The years passed gently, left it strong,*
*Though time began its quiet song.*

*A silver thread, here and there,*
*Whispered of wisdom beyond compare.*
*Yet still, his locks held youth's embrace,*
*Framing a face of timeless grace.*

*Not merely hair, but threads of soul,*
*That spoke of love and made us whole.*
*Each wave a story, each curl a sign,*
*Of the mercy sent through him, divine.*

## *The Eyes of the Beloved*

*His eyes, like stars in a midnight sky,*
*Large and bright, they never lied.*
*The whites gleamed pure, untarnished by strife,*
*Reflecting the beauty of a sacred life.*

*Dark pupils, deep as an ocean's core,*
*Pierced through hearts, forevermore.*
*A gaze so sharp, yet gentle and kind,*
*Carrying the strength of a soul refined.*

*Long lashes framed each thoughtful blink,*
*As if the world paused just to think.*
*In their shadows, mercy was found,*
*In their light, wisdom did abound.*

*When he looked, he saw beyond,*
*The fleeting world to the soul's true bond.*
*With every glance, compassion poured,*
*Strength in silence, love outpoured.*

*Eyes that held both hope and peace,*
*A solace where burdens found release.*
*They spoke with more than words could say,*
*Guiding lost hearts along the way.*

*O eyes that saw the truth so clear,*
*In their reflection, none need fear.*
*For they are the mirrors of a love untold,*
*A timeless mercy, gentle and bold.*

*The Ashrafiya Hymn*                *Dr. Ashi Ezz*

## The Brow of Grace, the Forehead of Light

Above his eyes, where wisdom lay,
His eyebrows arched in gentle sway.
Long and bold, they nearly met,
A graceful curve that none forget.

Yet in the center, a gap did part,
Like the space between dawn and dark.
A sign of balance, poised and pure,
His presence steady, calm, and sure.

His forehead broad, a beacon bright,
A symbol of leadership, glowing with light.
It shone with thought, with vision grand,
A mind that shaped both heart and land.

Beneath that brow, decisions rose,
Guiding the world as the river flows.
A noble glance, a thoughtful gleam,
The leader of truth, of the highest dream.

In every furrow, wisdom's grace did shine,
In every line, a trace of the divine.
Within your frame, the world was shown,
A face of peace, by light made known.

## The Nose of Grace, the Smile of Light

His nose, a curve so soft, so fine,
A subtle arch by Heaven's design.
In the middle, a gentle rise,
Like the crescent moon in twilight skies.

Yet more than form, it held a glow,
A light that only truth can show.
For in that face, so pure, so bright,
Was born the face of guiding light.

And his mouth, wide with words so true,
Spoke wisdom deep, that all hearts knew.
His teeth, like pearls, with gentle spacing aligned,
Each one a gem, each smile divine.

When he smiled, the world would gleam,
A warming touch, like a sunlit beam.
For in his lips, a kindness lay,
That turned the darkest night to day.

O mouth that spoke with grace untold,
O smile that made the timid bold.
In every space between his teeth,
A mercy shone, a joy beneath.

To see him smile was to see the stars,
To feel the peace that heals all scars.
His smile, a gift to those in need,
A silent prayer, a holy creed.

*So, when he laughed or simply grinned,*
*The hearts of men were gently pinned,*
*To hopes of love, to skies of grace,*
*For he was light in every face.*

## **The Beard of Majesty, The Neck of Grace**

A beard full and flowing, rich and neat,
Each strand a symbol, each thread complete.
Like rivers black under the moon's soft glow,
It framed his face with a humble show.

Not too long, nor too short it stood,
Trimmed with care, as only the noble would.
It carried wisdom, strength, and might,
A bearer of truth, a shield of light.

And in that beard, a hint of white,
Like stars that flicker in the night.
But age did not diminish his grace,
Only enhanced the beauty of his face.

His neck, long as sculptor's art,
A pillar pure, a flawless part.
Elegantly shaped, like silver bright,
Yet warm with life, a noble light.

Compared to silver, bright and clear,
It shone with purity, held so dear.
A sign of strength, of regal stance,
A beacon for every passing glance.

The Prophet's form, both strong and fine,
A perfect blend of the divine.
In every feature, nobility lay,
A light that guides, a path, a way.

## *Hands of Strength, Feet of Grace*

*His hands were strong, yet soft as the breeze,*
*Crafted with care, shaped to ease.*
*Large and firm, a gentle might,*
*That brought both comfort and pure delight.*

*In each warm touch, a calming peace,*
*A soothing balm, a sweet release.*
*His palms, like silk, yet firm as stone,*
*In every grip, his kindness shone.*

*With hands that healed, hands that gave,*
*A touch that knew how to uplift and save.*
*Whether on shoulder or clasped in greet,*
*A touch from him made hearts complete.*

*And his feet, as sturdy as the earth,*
*Rooted in strength, a mark of worth.*
*They walked through trials, deserts wide,*
*But never wavered, never strayed aside.*

*His steps were sure, his gait so light,*
*A reflection of his inner might.*
*In every stride, both grace and power,*
*A legacy built hour by hour.*

*Hands and feet, a perfect blend,*
*Of strength and love that never end.*
*In them, we see a Prophet's care,*
*Whose presence lifts, whose touch is rare.*

### *The Seal of Prophethood*

*Upon his neck, a sign was set,*
*A mark divine, none shall forget.*
*The Seal of Prophethood, raised and bright,*
*A mark that shone with heavenly light.*
*A symbol that his path was divine.*

*Jabir and Salman [91]saw it clear,*
*Between his shoulders, drawing near.*
*A mark like a pigeon's egg, they'd say,*
*A red, raised spot, glowing in its way.*
*They gazed in awe, with hearts at ease,*
*Knowing this seal was meant to please.*

*Abdullah spoke of how he'd yearned,*
*To see the seal, and how he learned,*
*The Prophet, sensing his desire,*
*Lifted his garment to inspire.*
*Around the mark, like freckles small,*
*A sight of wonder, loved by all.*

*So, in his beauty, seal, and grace,*
*Muhammad's light touched every face.*
*A Prophet pure, from head to heart,*
*With love and truth in every part.*

---

[91] Jabir ibn Samrah: A companion of Prophet Muhammad (PBUH).

## The Fragrance of Grace, The Gait of Command

A Prophet's grace in scent and stride,
With purpose sure, and love as guide.
He walked with presence, firm and strong,
Yet in his steps, no trace of wrong.

Without perfume, his essence stayed,
Like roses blooming in the shade.
Hands that touched him held the trace,
Of heavenly scent, a soft embrace.

When fragrance met his flawless skin,
It whispered of the light within.
A sweetness lingered, kind and clear,
A gift for all who ventured near.

His gait was like a steady breeze,
Descending slopes with perfect ease.
With purpose firm, he led the way,
Yet humbly stood, both night and day.

Leaning forward, stride by stride,
The earth beneath him seemed to glide.
A man of balance, grace, and might,
Who walked in peace, yet shone with light.

In every step, the world could see,
A soul both strong and truly free.
His fragrance filled the air, divine,
And in his walk, both strength and sign.

## *Beauty Made Complete*

*Ahmad; A beauty rare, untouched by time's decay,*
*A light eternal, guiding night and day.*
*In form, in heart, in soul, he stood apart,*
*A chosen leader, loved in every heart.*

*His form, a masterpiece, steady and bright,*
*A man of the earth, yet touched by might.*
*A pillar of calm, serene and keen,*
*The seal of Prophets, noble and seen.*

*A figure stood of noble, balanced grace,*
*With skin aglow, touched by a sunlit trace.*
*Unlike the pale, lifeless Roman hue,*
*His warmth was deep, luminous, steady view.*

*His hair, jet black, in gentle waves it fell,*
*Not bound too tight, nor loosed without a spell.*
*Each strand bespoke a care, a quiet pride,*
*A beauty simple, yet so magnified.*

*His face was round, his beard both full and neat,*
*His crescent brows above his lashes not meet.*
*His eyes, a radiant glow, so soft, so kind,*
*A steady warmth to calm the troubled mind.*

*His lips were set, with teeth as pearls aligned,*
*A smile to soothe and heal the heart confined.*
*His neck, like crafted silver jugs, stood tall,*
*A stately strength that held the gaze of all.*

*Of medium stature, yet towering high,*
*In hearts of those who saw him pass by.*

The Ashrafiya Hymn              Dr. Ashi Ezz

*Neither too tall nor too short, but grand,*
*A leader's presence, firm and planned.*

*Broad shoulders bore the world's great weight,*
*A chest of truth, steadfast and straight.*
*Muscular limbs, balanced and strong,*
*A frame for justice, righting the wrong.*

*His hands, though soft, had labored through the years,*
*Yet held the strength to quiet earthly fears.*
*His chest and stomach bore a gentle line,*
*A trace of care, both human and divine.*

*His legs stood firm, like patriarchs of yore,*
*His stride was sure, with purpose evermore.*
*Each step he took, a meaning to convey,*
*A path of patience, lighting all the way.*

*In any crowd, he stood so tall,*
*With dignity unmatched by all.*
*Grace in his stride, strength in his pace,*
*Elegance and power in perfect embrace.*

*A beauty rare, beyond compare,*
*With grace that lit the desert air.*
*A man whose presence held the night,*
*His face aglow with sacred light.*

*In every line, in every glance,*
*A wisdom deep, a soul's romance.*
*His features, balanced, bold, and bright,*
*Reflected heaven's purest light.*

*His stature held both strength and ease,*
*With dignity that bent the breeze.*

The Ashrafiya Hymn

Dr. Ashi Ezz

*Yet all who saw him felt at peace,*
*In awe, but love could never cease.*

*His moral compass, shining through,*
*Made every movement pure and true.*
*No force could dim the light he bore,*
*A guide, a beacon, evermore.*

*Companions spoke of light so clear,*
*That in his smile, joy drew near.*
*A brightness not just skin-deep shown,*
*But from his spirit, fully grown.*

*Approachable, yet firm and wise,*
*Authority within his eyes.*
*You couldn't help but love his grace,*
*When light from him would fill a space.*

*Muhammad, beauty made complete,*
*A love profound, a bond so sweet.*
*With every glance, with every word,*
*The heart is stirred, the soul is heard.*

*For in his face, a light so pure,*
*That only love could be the cure.*
*To see him was to love him true,*
*For through him, heaven's essence flew.*

## *Your Love for Him Must Conquer Even Death*

By God, who holds the soul of Muhammad near,
None of you believe unless it's clear:
More than father, son, or life's sweet breath,
Your love for him must conquer even death.

For God has sent him as a mercy bright,
A guiding star, a light in the night.
Not for one people, but for all mankind,
A mercy to the worlds, both just and kind.

In tenderness, his heart was shaped by grace,
No stubborn pride, no harshness in his face.
Had he been cold or hard in heart and tone,
The people near him would have leave him alone.

But God bestowed on him a gentle might,
A soul that pardons, turning wrong to right.
He prayed for those astray, forgave their sin,
And sought their trust to draw their hearts within.

When Lord took root within his soul,
He placed in God's great hands his final goal.
A mercy sent to heal, unite, and guide,
In love and faith, his people now abide.

But tell me, are you blind, or deaf, or lost?
To see his light and not love him is cost.
If knowledge of his grace stirs not your heart,
What arrogance or folly plays its part?

*The Ashrafiya Hymn*                                                           *Dr. Ashi Ezz*

**The End**

# The Book Cover

The cover speaks a timeless tale of light and guidance, where the moon becomes a radiant symbol of Prophet Muhammad (PBUH), leading humanity toward enlightenment and salvation. Majestic and all-encompassing, the moon reflects the Prophet's wisdom, compassion, and teachings, illuminating the path through the vast desert of life's trials. Its celestial glow pierces the darkness, offering hope and purpose to those lost in shadows of despair.

The lone traveler, steady and humble, embodies humanity. The staff in his hand is not just a tool but a symbol of faith, resilience, and trust in divine guidance. His journey across the barren dunes mirrors life's struggles; the tests of endurance, patience, and belief in what lies beyond. Yet, he moves forward, drawn by the moon's gentle light, representing the Prophet's teachings leading souls toward paradise.

The desert, vast and unyielding, symbolizes life's hardships, a realm of impermanence and spiritual awakening. The play of light and shadow on the dunes reflects moments of clarity and struggle, reminding us of the balance between trials and faith. Together, the moon and the traveler craft a profound narrative: the Prophet, like the radiant moon, shines endlessly, guiding humanity through life's desert toward the eternal oasis of paradise.

# Acknowledgments

I give all praise to Allah for finishing this book; beneath the heavens, vast and wide, in every breath, His signs abide. The sun that rises, the stars that gleam, the rivers that flow, the mountains supreme. His mercy endless, His wisdom profound, in every atom, His wonders are found. He shaped the earth, He gave us sight, our guide through darkness, the eternal Light. With Him, I possess everything; without Him, I am left with nothing.

Upon this earth, He sent a man, the Seal of the Prophets, the perfect plan. Muhammad, whose words in hearts reside, a beacon of truth, a nation's guide. With him stood souls, both strong and pure, the Companions' faith, steadfast and sure. And through the ages, scholars came, preserving wisdom, spreading His name. From pen to tongue, the knowledge flowed, a legacy bright where truth has glowed.

Now AI aids with thoughtful care, editing words to make them fair and enhance readability.

# References

Al-Jazuli, M. (2007). Dalail al-Khayrat. Dar Al Kotob Al Ilmiyah.

Al-Mubarakpuri, S. (1996). Ar-Raheeq Al-Makhtum (The Sealed Nectar): Biography of the Noble Prophet (Revised Edition). Dar-us-Salam Publications.

Al-Samarkandi, A. H. (1998). Kitab al-Samarkandiyya. Dar al-Minhaj.

Al-Tirmidhi, M. I. (2008). Al-Shamā'il al-Muhammadiyya (A. Bewley, Trans.). Diwan Press.

Al-Yahsubi, Q. A. (2003). Ash-Shifa bi Ta'rif Huquq al-Mustafa (A. Bewley, Trans.). Madinah Press.

Bukhari, M. I. (1997). *Sahih Bukhari* (M. M. Khan, Trans.). Dar-us-Salam Publications.

Ezz, Ashi. (2024). *Muhammad: Lasting Resilience Model*. [Available on Amazon: https://a.co/d/e7hR0rB]. ISBN: 978-1-0670358-3-9.

Ibn Hisham, A. M. (2009). Al-Sirah al-Nabawiyyah (S. Guillaume, Trans.). Oxford University Press.

Kandhlawi, M. Z. (2004). Fada'il al-A'mal (M. A. Elias, Trans.). Kutub Khana Ishayat-ul-Islam.

The Qur'an. (1999). (M. T. Al-Hilali & M. M. Khan, Trans.). King Fahd Complex for the Printing of the Holy Qur'an.